8 May 2008

Heard by Me

Heard by Me

Essays on My Buddhist Teacher

by

Shūichi Maida

Edited and Translated

with an Introduction and Notes

by

Nobuo Haneda

FROG PRESS

1992

Berkeley, California

The calligraphy on the cover is "Thus Have I Heard" (*Nyo-ze Ga Mon*) by Shūichi Maida.

Frog Press
P.O. Box 9670
Berkeley, CA 94709-0670

First Edition, 1992

Library of Congress Catalog Card Number: 90-082529

ISBN 0-9627231-0-X

Printed in the United States of America

Rev. Akegarasu is always whispering in my ear, "There is nothing to worry about. You had better do whatever you want to do." This is the Buddha-Dharma that I heard from him.

— Shūichi Maida

Contents

Translator's Introduction

In this book I have selected and translated twenty-two essays by Shūichi Maida (1906–67), one of the most important Buddhist thinkers of modern Japan. In these essays Maida talks about his teacher, the Rev. Haya Akegarasu (1877–1954). More specifically, he discusses his relationship with Akegarasu and the essence of the man's teachings.

At the age of eighteen, Maida heard Rev. Akegarasu speak and was so much impressed by Akegarasu's personality and teaching that the entire course of his life was changed. Akegarasu was the first person who seemed to him an image of the Buddha, an ideal human being. Maida, to use his own words, "fell in love with the Buddha." As the years went by, this love intensified.

When Maida first heard Akegarasu, he was a high school student in his home town of Kanazawa in Ishikawa Prefecture majoring in science. He lost interest in science and started to read books on religion and philosophy. He then entered the University of Kyoto and studied Western philosophy under Kitarō Nishida (1870–1945), one of the most eminent philosophers in modern Japan. But then Maida lost interest in academic learning altogether and wanted to leave the university to pursue the way of a religious seeker. His parents strongly opposed this idea and advised him to finish his studies. As a compromise, Maida, when he was a senior, spent seven months in Shiono Misaki, a seaside village at the southern end of the island of Honshū, swimming, reading, and meditating.

1

In 1929, when he was twenty-three, he graduated from the university. The following year, after two months of military service, he was honorably discharged because of a knee injury that he had suffered as a child. He then became a teacher at Kanazawa Daisan Junior High School. At age thirty-one, after serving as a junior high school teacher for seven years, he became a professor at the Teachers' College in Nagano Prefecture. He taught at the college for five years, during which time he deepened his understanding of Buddhism by studying many Buddhist texts and thinkers. He regularly held a study class at his home that some of his students attended.

In 1942, during World War II, Maida moved back to his home town from Nagano and became a professor at Ishikawa Teachers' College for Women. In the same year he accompanied Prof. Gyōshō Shimizu, the president of the Teachers' College and a student of Rev. Akegarasu, on a visit to Rev. Akegarasu at his temple in Kita-yasuda in Ishikawa Prefecture. Thus nineteen years after he first heard Akegarasu, he met him personally for the first time. Maida then realized that the most important objective in his life was to learn from Akegarasu. He started to attend Akegarasu's seminars.

When World War II ended, Maida felt a strong inner urge to change his life. In letters addressed to his former students in Nagano, Maida expressed his desire to go back to Nagano and do nothing but study the teachings of Akegarasu with them. Some students in Nagano responded favorably to this idea.

On January 6, 1946, Maida, who had already decided to return to Nagano and leave his job and family in his home town, visited Akegarasu at his temple. When Maida told Akegarasu about his intention of going to Nagano and engaging in Buddhist activities there, the teacher strongly encouraged him to do so. The next day, Maida left for Nagano leaving everything behind.

From that day until he passed away on February 27, 1967, for twenty-one years, Maida lived in Nagano, studying Buddhism with his students. Probably very few individuals in Buddhist history ever engaged in such dynamic learning activities as Maida did during those twenty-one years. Learning from Akegarasu and sharing his teachings with others became his whole life. Every year Maida invited

Akegarasu to Nagano for lectures. He also regularly attended Akegarasu's seminars at the teacher's temple.

From 1947 to 1951 Maida wrote and published many essays in *Truth*, his monthly journal. In 1952, he became the managing editor of *Great Assembly*, Akegarasu's monthly journal. He also edited Akegarasu's other writings until the teacher passed away in 1954.

At this time, some students of Akegarasu hoped that Maida would become their teacher. But Maida considered it against Akegarasu's teachings to lead a group in the teacher's name, and he severed his ties with those students and resigned his editorship of *Great Assembly*. In the following year Maida started publication of *Mt. Himalaya*, his own monthly journal, which lasted until he passed away in 1967, totaling 148 issues.

In 1966, a year before he himself died, Maida (1) published a revised text of the *Bandō-bon* (i.e., Shinran's own handwritten version) of the *Kyōgyōshinshō*; (2) criticized such scholars as Dr. Kitarō Nishida, Dr. Daisetz T. Suzuki [1870–1966, a Zen scholar], and Rev. Dai'ei Kaneko [1881–1976, a Shin scholar]; and (3) wrote the *Face to Face with Śākyamuni*, a commentary on the *Sutta-Nipāta*, one of the oldest Buddhist scriptures. Maida did the first in order to provide a reliable basic text for the translation of the *Kyōgyōshinshō* into several foreign languages, something which Akegarasu had strongly desired. He did the second because he wanted to show the uniqueness of Akegarasu by distinguishing him from other scholars. He did the third because he, as the title of the book indicates, wanted to see Śākyamuni face to face. In Maida's mind Śākyamuni and Akegarasu were one.

At the end of the year, Maida wrote the essay "Rev. Akegarasu and Rev. Kiyozawa." In it he described the great happiness he had experienced on meeting Akegarasu:

> I was able to see Rev. Akegarasu. For me, there is no Buddha-Dharma apart from him. He is the Buddha-Dharma. He is Śākyamuni himself. If this idea is a mistake, then all of my life has been a mistake. It is, however, all right. I could die with satisfaction.

In his New Year's resolution of 1967, his final year, Maida stated, "I want to write a biography of Rev. Akegarasu." Thus he started to write some essays about Akegarasu and publish them in his journal. But his desire to write his teacher's biography was not realized because he passed away in February of that year.

Maida left a voluminous amount of writing. His complete works comprise more than ten thousand pages, most of which were written in the last twenty-one years of his life. Yet it is not an exaggeration to say that it is all commentary on Akegarasu's teachings.

This present book has three parts. Part One consists of ten essays in which Maida discusses his personal relationship with Akegarasu.

Part Two consists of ten essays in which he talks about the teacher-student relationship in a more general manner. These are included because this translator hopes that they will help the reader to gain a deeper understanding of the essays in Part One.

Part Three consists of two essays on what Maida considers the most essential teachings of Akegarasu. The first comments on the teacher's statement, "The flame from the cremation of my entire self is my only liberation," the second on his statement, "I am the devil."

Since the teacher-student relationship is the theme of this book, a discussion of Maida's views on this relationship is in order, particularly on the following seven points:

    I.   The importance of having a teacher in Buddhism;
    II.   The teacher embodies the truth of impermanence;
   III. The teacher is a true student;
   IV. The teacher is a guide, not a goal;
    V.   The teacher works as absolute negation;
   VI. The teacher actualizes freedom, independence, and creativity in the student;
  VII. The true teacher can be recognized only after the liberation experience.

I. The Importance of Having a Teacher in Buddhism

In any kind of artistic or academic training we must have a teacher who excels in the field. But nowhere is a teacher so crucial as in Buddhism. From his association with his teacher, Maida knew that meeting with a teacher and learning from him is the most important thing in a person's life. He says:

> The most important problem in the sphere of the human spirit is, after all, whether one meets with a teacher or not. The focal point is whether one meets with a real human being, a real personality.
>
> ("Learn Freedom!")

Maida believed that without meeting Akegarasu, he could not have understood Buddhism. For him, Buddhism consisted not in learning abstract concepts but in facing an actual human being:

> It is totally useless to read books, sūtras, commentaries, or sayings and judge them by one's arbitrary tastes. Unless all of our human positions are completely smashed to pieces by one person, by a spiritual guide, we cannot possibly understand the subjective nothingness of Śākyamuni. Some people may say that we can understand nothingness only through our intellectual understanding. But unfortunately, that is not real, subjective nothingness. It is absolutely impossible to touch subjective nothingness without meeting with a spiritual guide.
>
> ("Reflections on the Teacher-Student Relationship")

The importance of having a specific personal teacher is stressed by the two major Buddhist traditions in Japan, Shin and Zen.

Shinran (1173–1262), the founder of Shin Buddhism, believed that his predecessors had transmitted the teachings of their respective predecessors. Shinran himself regarded Hōnen (1133–1212), the founder of the Japanese Pure Land School, as his personal teacher. He often stated that without Hōnen, he could not have understood Buddhism.

Yuienbō, a disciple of Shinran, described the essence of the Shin Buddhist tradition as follows:

> How can we enter the path of the Easy Practice [i.e., Shin Buddhism] if we do not rely upon a teacher whom we meet in our life?[1]

Zen also emphasizes the importance of the transmission of the teaching from teacher to student. For example, Dōgen (1200–53), the founder of the Japanese Sōtō Zen School, was a student of the Zen master Ju-ching (1163–1228). Dōgen asserted:

> If you do not have a true teacher, you had better not study Buddhism.[2]

The Rev. Haya Akegarasu also considered his meeting with the Rev. Manshi Kiyozawa [1863–1903, a Shin thinker][3] the most important event in his life. He devoted his entire life to learning from him. He stressed the importance of having one personal teacher:

> Both those who have many teachers and those who have no teacher have not yet discovered their own way.
>
> Both those who worship many gods and Buddhas and those who worship no god and no Buddha have not yet discovered the world of truth.
>
> Blessed are those who have only one teacher, who serve only one Buddha![4]

We can say that Buddhism has been maintained only in the teacher-student relationship. Or it would be more accurate to say that the teacher-student relationship itself is Buddhism. It is when we have a personal teacher, when we become a student, that Buddhism exists for us. Let us now examine what the teacher is in Buddhism.

II. The Teacher Embodies the Truth of Impermanence

What, then, does the teacher embody? According to Maida, he embodies impermanence, which is the ultimate truth taught by Śākyamuni. In order to understand this aspect of the teacher, we must review the life of Śākyamuni, particularly his awakening experience, because he is the historical prototype for the teacher in Buddhism.

Tradition tells us that Śākyamuni was originally a prince in a small kingdom in Northwest India. After learning the inevitability of old age, sickness, and death, he left his home and became a religious seeker at twenty-nine. Then he spent the next six years learning the traditional religions and practicing the most intense ascetic practice, but he could not find the ultimate peace for which he was searching. Then he meditated under a tree with the determination not to move from the spot until he had attained awakening.

What, then, was the content of his meditation? In his meditation he examined whether there was anything permanent in his being. First he looked into his physical existence and realized that all the things that made up his body were constantly moving and flowing. Next he searched his mind, thinking that it was there that the *ātman* (permanent self or soul) could be found. Although he desperately searched for it, he could not discover it. Thus he finally concluded that his mind consisted of the four aggregates—sensation, conception, volition, and consciousness—and that all these were constantly moving and changing. Then one morning when he saw the morning star, he attained awakening and became an Awakened One, a Buddha.[5]

What was the content of Śākyamuni's awakening? It was insight into the truth of impermanence. In Buddhism, the word *Dharma* refers to impermanence, the ultimate truth. He understood that since all things in the universe are constantly moving, changing, and flowing, it is a mistake to presuppose an eternal entity like the *ātman*. Thus the truth of impermanence totally destroyed what he considered his "self"; it emptied him. Then the truth permeated him and he became one with it.

Śākyamuni described the content of his awakening thus:

My life is already spent. The Holy Work is already established.[6]

Here the twofold—negative and positive—aspect of his awakening experience is mentioned. The first sentence indicates that the truth of impermanence, here a negative power, has destroyed everything he cherished. He recognized the impossibility of maintaining any idea, thought, opinion, self-love, or self-pride. In this realization, he experienced spiritual death.[7] The second sentence describes how the same truth, here a positive force that he now calls the Holy Work, has brought a wondrous reality into his life. He now sees this world as a constantly new, creative world, and all existing things in it as its creative components. In this realization he experienced spiritual rebirth.

Thus his statements show that he became a truly humble person (because impermanence shattered everything in him); and that he became a truly dynamic person (because the same truth opened up a free, exuberant, and creative life for him). Embodying the truth, Śākyamuni lived a humble and dynamic life. Here it is important to note that the core of Buddhism is *how* Śākyamuni lived, not his thoughts or ideas. Buddhism spread, and many people took refuge in it, mainly because of Śākyamuni's humble and dynamic spiritual qualities.

Maida saw the same spiritual qualities in Akegarasu; he saw the truth of impermanence in him. When the 18-year-old Maida attended one of Akegarasu's lectures for the first time, he was astounded by the teacher. As soon as Akegarasu came into the hall and sat in a chair, he shouted, "Those of you who have brought pencils and paper with you, leave immediately!" Then the teacher told the audience that the important thing in Buddhism is a "flash," not an idea to be recorded or memorized. Maida says:

> What kind of truth did Śākyamuni discover in this world? He discovered one truth, and he called it "impermanence." Impermanence is something you cannot grasp. If you can grasp a thing, it is no longer impermanent ... Thus if there is anything that is fixed, there cannot be any truth of impermanence. This truth can only be described as a "flash."
>
> ... Thus I heard directly from him [Akegarasu] that truth is a flash. Pointing at his forehead, he taught us, "If you have a sharp flash of truth during the course of my talk, that's it. Then you have not wasted your time by attending my lectures for three evenings."
>
> When I listened to these words, I felt as if everything I had cherished was completely taken away from me.
>
> ("Meeting with Impermanence")

Maida says that a good grasp of the truth of impermanence is essential for understanding Akegarasu, because the teacher was an embodiment of the truth:

> Rev. Akegarasu was not a preacher who looked solemn or serious. He never said "O.K." to his small, limited self. Far from affirming his self, he kept on smashing his selves one after another, moment by moment. He never stayed in one place for even a second ... He did not possess anything. Far from possessing things in this world, he was continuously throwing away, one after the other, those selves that possessed something ... In living such a life as his, one becomes the truth of impermanence itself. Rev. Akegarasu was an embodiment of impermanence—the truth that Śākyamuni taught.
>
> ("The Crucial Essence of Shinshū")

The teacher in Buddhism embodies the truth of impermanence and manifests it. The only thing the student must learn from him is the truth. Maida devoted his entire life to learning it from the teacher.

III.   The Teacher Is a True Student

We have said that Śākyamuni, the historical prototype for the teacher, was permeated with the truth of impermanence. Since the truth is a dynamically advancing force, its penetration into a human existence means that one becomes a dynamic seeker, a student. The life-style of a student is the only possible life-style for a person who is permeated with the truth. Thus it would be more accurate to say that Śākyamuni became a student, rather than a teacher, at the moment of his awakening.

Thus impermanence and studentship are synonymous; the former is the truth itself and the latter is the form the truth takes when it is converted into a human life-style. Just as we are emancipated when we are penetrated by the truth of impermanence, so we are liberated when we live true studentship. Realizing true studentship is not one of the conditions for liberation in Buddhism; it is the content of liberation.

Since the student spirit is the core of Buddhism, we can say that Buddhism is a tradition of individuals who have identified themselves as students. All authentic Buddhists have regarded themselves as students; none of them have claimed to be a teacher. In that sense, no teacher has ever existed in Buddhist history.

But is it not the case that some Buddhists are called teachers in Buddhism? What, then, is a teacher in Buddhism? A person who is called a teacher is actually a perfect student. The person who embodies perfect studentship is a model for those who aspire to be like him. Such a person is called a teacher by those aspirants. Simply because such a model is *more of a student* than the aspirants, he is regarded by them as their teacher. Thus teachership exists *only in the mind of the student*; it never exists in the mind of the model person. If the person who is called a teacher were to regard himself as a teacher, he would be too conceited to be a model student.

Throughout Buddhist history Buddhists aspired to the perfect studentship that they saw in their teachers. The goal of their learning was perfect studentship. Thus the terms Buddha and perfect student are synonyms. So-called Buddhas are all perfect students—humble and dynamic seekers.

Here a few words concerning the difference between the two Buddhas Śākyamuni and Amida are in order. Śākyamuni, as we have seen, was the historical prototype for perfect studentship, whereas Amida is a symbolic (or universal) prototype for perfect studentship, which was developed by the ancient Indians after the passing of Śākyamuni. The basic source for the idea of Amida is a text called the *Larger Sukhāvatīvyūha-sūtra*, in which a student by the name of Dharmākara (or Hōzō in Japanese) symbolizes the spirit of a constant seeker. When he fulfills his Buddhahood (or perfect studentship), he becomes a Buddha by the name of Amitābha, Amida in Japanese.

In Pure Land Buddhism, Amida's full name is *Namu-Amida-Butsu* (Bowing-Infinite-Awakened). This name means that he is awakened (*Butsu*) to the infinite (*Amida*) because of his bowing (*Namu*). Thus Amida, or *Namu-Amida-Butsu*, is a symbol for the humble (with which the term *Namu* [bowing] is synonymous) and dynamic (with which the term *Amida* [infinite] is synonymous) student spirit.

There is another important concept in the Pure Land tradition. It is called *shinjin* (genuine trust).[8] It refers to a student's union with

Amida's student spirit. When a student encounters Amida's spirit and, being moved by it, becomes one with it, he experiences liberation. The expression of his heartfelt gratitude—recitation of Amida's name (*Namu-Amida-Butsu*)—is called the *nembutsu*.

The Pure Land masters considered *shinjin* (or *nembutsu*) the most important thing in Buddhism, because they experienced liberation in it. For example, Hōnen experienced liberation when he saw Amida's spirit in Shan-tao's (613–81, a Chinese Pure Land master) writings and became one with it by becoming Shan-tao's student. Hōnen's motto was "exclusive reliance upon Shan-tao."

Likewise, Shinran experienced liberation when he witnessed Amida in Hōnen and became his student. The same thing happened to individuals such as Yuienbō; they were liberated when they saw the humble spirit in Shinran and identified themselves as his students.

Although some people called Shinran their teacher, Shinran never considered himself their teacher nor those people as his disciples; he called them fellow learners and fellow practitioners. His humble self-identification as only a student is clearly expressed in the statement: "I do not have even a single disciple."[9]

In modern Japan, Akegarasu revered Kiyozawa as his teacher because he saw Amida in him. Kiyozawa lived his relatively short life of forty years in constant search of truth. When he told Akegarasu, "Never preach even if you die!," he taught the student never to become a teacher and to stay a student throughout his life. Akegarasu kept this admonition and lived his life only as a student.

It was this perfect studentship—the truth translated into a human life-style—that the eighteen-year-old Maida saw in Akegarasu. Maida was overwhelmed by the teacher's humble and dynamic spirit. His life after the meeting was a process by which he learned the studentship that he saw in the teacher.

IV.   The Teacher Is a Guide, Not a Goal

Although we have been emphasizing the importance of the teacher, we must note here that the teacher is a guide, not a goal. He helps the student to attain the truth, or perfect studentship.

Like an extension chord that connects an electric appliance with electricity but cannot claim to generate the energy, the teacher connects the student to the truth but cannot claim to have invented the truth.

Although Śākyamuni is mistakenly regarded by some people as a liberator, he was actually a *liberated* person and did not claim to be a liberator. Instead, he emphasized that the truth awakened and liberated him. Hence, his famous message on his deathbed: "Don't make any human being your refuge! Make the Dharma your refuge!"[10]

Maida stresses the importance of seeing the truth in the teacher, not his human qualities:

> So-called "inappropriate reliance on the teacher" occurs when one does not see the Dharma in the teacher. The Dharma is the most important thing in the teacher, not his personality or human qualities ... We must immediately go to the Dharma that the teacher embodies. We must see the Dharma, not the person ...
>
> Here the Dharma is the great life of the universe. This is what we should pay attention to. This is what we should rely upon. It is not a person. The teacher does not tell us, "Come to me!" He always tells us, "Go to the Dharma through me!" We should not forget this even for a second. The teacher is a breakthrough opening through which the Dharma—the life of the universe—contacts us.
>
> ("The Words of the Good Person")

The essence of the teacher is impermanence, or perfect studentship. The truth has liberated the teacher and is what the teacher desires to share with the student. Thus when the student is finally led to the truth and becomes one with it, both the teacher and the student are totally one; they both engage in the same dynamic learning activities. There is no longer any dualistic relationship between teacher and student. Neither is there any room for the student's attachment to the teacher.

In the following short poem, Akegarasu described the ultimate sphere where there is no longer any teacher-student relationship, only the truth:

> There is no "my Dharma" to be transmitted.
> There is no "my student," either.
> There are only the stars twinkling in the high sky.
>
> ("Rev. Akegarasu and Rev. Kiyozawa")

Maida appreciated Akegarasu because the teacher guided him to impermanence, to true studentship. Akegarasu did not allow Maida to be attached to him. Maida says that Akegarasu did not behave like a teacher, nor did he treat Maida as his student. The teacher lived only as a student and just hoped that Maida would also live as a student, recognizing the truth and becoming one with it.

Thus the main task of the teacher is to enable the student to become truly independent—even from the teacher; he enjoys being what he is. We shall discuss the independence that the teacher realizes in the student in Section VI.

V.   The Teacher Works as Absolute Negation

We have discussed the twofold—negative and positive—function of the truth of impermanence. Since the teacher embodies the truth, his function is also twofold: negation and affirmation. In this section we shall expound on the teacher's negative function toward the student. In the next section, we shall examine his positive (or affirmative) function.

The teacher works as negation to a student who is attached to his possessions. He challenges, negates, and takes away everything that the student cherishes. This was precisely what the eighteen-year-old Maida experienced in his first meeting with Akegarasu.

Maida calls the teacher's negation an authentic religious experience:

> Truly meeting with a teacher means only one thing: that one's personality is entirely smashed to pieces before that person. Could there be any authentic religious experience apart from the experience of having one's personality totally blown away? Religious experiences that are conceived in the heads of scholars have no meaning whatsoever.
>
> ("Reflections on the Teacher-Student Relationship")

Maida talks about the negation that existed between Hōnen and Shinran. He claims that without it Shinran would not have become Shinran:

13

> Shinran studied under Hōnen for three years. How harshly, how devilishly, Hōnen must have crushed Shinran during this period, day after day, moment after moment! Thinking about this, I cannot help trembling. But without that, Shinran the independent person would not have been born. It was because Shinran's personality was completely crushed by Hōnen that Shinran respected him as the teacher in his life.
>
> > ("Reflections on the Teacher-Student Relationship")

Maida talks about the similar "crushing" of Akegarasu by Kiyozawa:

> Rev. Akegarasu was crushed by the spiritual hammer of the Rev. Manshi Kiyozawa day after day, night after night, for three years while he was living in the Kōkō-dō dormitory in Tokyo. Never, not even once, did Rev. Kiyozawa express approval of Akegarasu's ideas.
>
> > ("Standing-Death")

Further, Maida talks about the total negation which he himself experienced from Akegarasu in such essays as "Standing-Death" and "Rev. Akegarasu and Rev. Kiyozawa."

Maida believes that this crushing was the most important thing in his life. It made him understand the futility of everything he cherished, be it pride, thoughts, or ideas. It made him see the meaninglessness of his being itself. In short, it made him humble. It also made him dynamic. Let us now discuss the affirmative aspect of the teacher's challenge.

VI.   The Teacher Actualizes Freedom, Independence, and Creativity in the Student

The teacher deprives the student of all his nonessential coatings. However, his negative action simultaneously brings out the deepest reality in the student. Maida says,

> Through his association with Rev. Kiyozawa, Rev. Akegarasu was purified. The original and shining Akegarasu was revealed by Kiyozawa.
>
> > ("Rev. Akegarasu and Rev. Kiyozawa")

When the student has his own "original and shining" nature revealed by the teacher, his life is characterized by many positive spiritual

14

declared, "My denomination is the Akegarasu School. The only follower is myself. There is no need whatsoever to spread it." He powerfully shouted, "In the heavens and on the earth *my aloneness* is noble." Rev. Akegarasu lived his life all by himself.

("Rev. Akegarasu and Rev. Kiyozawa")

Being freed from all relative values of the world and liberated into his own absolutely unique world, Akegarasu became a truly independent person.

Maida bore deep in his mind the importance of becoming an independent person. He treaded the path to independence, following the example of his teacher.

C. Creativity

Maida emphasizes the importance of learning as the basis for creativity. It is only after one has thoroughly learned from his teacher that he can create something new. Maida says,

> Quiet listening and careful thinking about what one has heard is the only thing that can make a person take a creative first step without any effort. More emphasis should be placed on learning than on thinking new ideas. Creativity comes quite naturally out of learning.

("Learn Freedom!")

Maida calls the final stage of spiritual development the stage of personal attainment,[12] in which one steps into a world uniquely his own. Maida characterizes it as the stage in which "one attains awakening alone, without a teacher."[13] This traditional phrase, Maida claims, does not mean that a teacher is unimportant, but that the student, having thoroughly learned from the teacher, develops a world uniquely his own. Maida believes that all great individuals, such as Śākyamuni and Shinran, attained awakening alone, without a teacher. For example, Maida says of Shinran,

> Shinran's predecessors formed the world of his awakening. And he, having totally embraced those predecessors, stood up in his own awakening as an independent personality ... Shinran, having thoroughly learned from his Pure Land predecessors

17

and gone beyond them, developed his own unique world of awakening.

("On History")

Shinran was a faithful student of Hōnen throughout his life. This, however, does not mean that he blindly copied the teacher's understanding of Buddhism. On the contrary, Shinran's thorough investigation of the teacher's teachings enabled him to create a unique spiritual world.

Similarly, Kiyozawa, Akegarasu, and Maida, sharing the same spirit of a humble student, learned from their respective teachers and developed their own unique spiritual worlds.[14]

VII.   The True Teacher Can Be Recognized Only After the Liberation Experience

The final issue to be discussed here concerns the *true* teacher. When we emphasize the importance of a teacher, there immediately arises the question "How can we tell who is a true teacher?" Maida answers,

> Can I, on my part, tell whether a certain person is a true teacher or not? Can I, for example, select a true teacher from three candidates, Mr. A, Mr. B, and Mr. C? The truth of the matter is that I do not yet understand what is true. How, then, can I, who do not yet understand what is true, determine whether a certain teacher is true or not? It is a mistake typical of a person who thinks in terms of objective logic to believe that he can choose a true teacher from several candidates by comparing and evaluating them.
>
> ("The Most Important Thing in My Life")

If one is selecting a contest winner out of several candidates, one may be able to rely upon his own judgement. But in evaluating a teacher, a human being who is greater than himself, the student cannot use his own deluded criteria. How could he tell who the true teacher is by a deluded measure that must be destroyed by the teacher? Maida discusses how this point applies to Shinran:

> Since Shinran's eyes are totally muddled by desires and passions, the image of Hōnen reflected in his eyes is unclear and blurred.

18

> Since Shinran wears a pair of colored glasses, the Hōnen whom
> he sees is of the same color.
>
> ("Even If I Were To Be Deceived")

Shinran cannot use his own "colored glasses" to judge the true teacher.
Whomever he sees is already tainted by the color of his bias.

Then is there nothing by which we can judge who the true teacher
is? Maida says that there is one thing—the student's oneness with the
teacher, or *shinjin*. This oneness means that the student, whose self
has been totally negated and embraced by the teacher, has become one
with him; and that the student can no longer tell whether the teacher
is true or false. Only the existence of this oneness, not the student's
judgement, can prove that his teacher is the true teacher for him.
Maida says:

> It is not because we regard a person as a true teacher that a true
> teacher exists. That a person is a true teacher is spontaneously
> revealed ... when the student and the teacher are one, and the
> student cannot tell whether his teacher is true or false.
>
> ("Even If I Were To Be Deceived")

Thus as far as Shinran is concerned, only his oneness with Hōnen can
prove that Hōnen was the true teacher for him. In other words, only
the existence of a true *student* can prove that there is a true teacher for
him. We can see Shinran's oneness with the teacher in his words,

> The good person [Hōnen] said, "Just say the *nembutsu* and be
> liberated by Amida Buddha." As far as I, Shinran, am concerned,
> I just accept and trust his words. That's all.
>
> I am totally ignorant as to whether the *nembutsu* is truly the
> cause of my attaining birth in the Pure Land or whether it is a
> karmic action because of which I must fall into Hell. Even if I
> were to be deceived by Hōnen Shōnin, even if I were to fall into
> Hell because of saying the *nembutsu*, I would not regret it.[15]

We can see the same oneness in Maida. From his first meeting with
the teacher at eighteen to his own death, for over forty years, Maida
kept on deepening his understanding of the teacher. In the passage
quoted earlier, which he wrote two months before his death, Maida
said:

> I was able to see Rev. Akegarasu. For me, there is no Buddha-Dharma apart from him. He is the Buddha-Dharma. He is Śākyamuni himself. If this idea is a mistake, then all of my life has been a mistake. It is, however, all right. I could die with satisfaction.

This statement shows Maida's *shinjin*; his entire life was spent in learning from the teacher and he feels deep joy and happiness about it. It also shows that Maida lived the life of a true student and that Akegarasu was a true teacher for him.

In this book Japanese names are given in Western order, surnames last. Material in square brackets has been inserted into the translations for clarity.

All notes are the translator's. The bibliography contains selected Japanese and English works concerning Haya Akegarasu, Manshi Kiyozawa, and Shūichi Maida. For further bibliographical information concerning Manshi Kiyozawa, see *December Fan*, pp. 95–8.

I am deeply indebted to the Rev. Gyōkō Saitō, Bishop of Higashi Honganji of North America, for the theme of this book. It was his book *Shout of Buddha* as well as his guidance that inspired me to write this book.

I am also deeply indebted to friends who helped me complete this project. First, I wish to express my sincere gratitude to Steve Kaufman for reading the manuscript several times and giving me valuable suggestions. I am also indebted to Diane Ames and Brian Galloway, whose excellent editorial skills have improved the content of this work. I also wish to express my thanks to Joan Sweany, who edited my translations when they first appeared in the bulletins of the Buddhist Temple of Chicago.

I am grateful to Mr. Shigeharu Watanabe, Maida's student, for letting me use Maida's calligraphy for the cover of this book. The four Chinese characters (*Nyo-ze Ga Mon*) mean "Thus Have I Heard." This is the Chinese translation of the Sanskrit phrase, *Evaṃ mayā śrutam* (thus heard by me). All Buddhist sūtras begin with this phrase. Since this expression seems to me to describe the essence of Buddhism, which is studentship, better than any other, I have used it as the title of this book.

And last, but not least, my sincere thanks to my wife Tomoko for encouraging me in this project. If she had not, this book would not have been completed.

Nobuo Haneda
Berkeley, California
June 12, 1991

PART ONE

My Buddhist Teacher, Rev. Akegarasu

1

Meeting with Impermanence

I am from the city of Kanazawa in Ishikawa Prefecture. A Buddhist teacher by the name of Haya Akegarasu lived near Kanazawa. You may have heard of him. He was a Shin Buddhist minister. It has been thirteen years since he passed away; this year we will hold his thirteenth [special] memorial service. I first learned about Buddhism, particularly the teaching of Shinran, from Rev. Akegarasu. Thus I can only talk about Buddhism from the standpoint of Rev. Akegarasu's teaching.

After graduating from a four-year junior high school, I entered the science department of Shikō High School with the intention of eventually studying electrical engineering in a university. When I was a sophomore in high school, however, I attended a lecture by Rev. Akegarasu in the Kanazawa city hall. He talked about the "Verses in Praise of a Buddha"[1] in the *Larger Sukhāvatīvyūha-sūtra*, one of the Mahāyāna sūtras.

As I reflect back, I can say that my life was completely turned around by listening to Rev. Akegarasu. I lost interest in studying. When I graduated from high school, my parents told me, "Since you have been to a high school, you might as well continue your education at a university." So, since I could not find anything else to do, I entered the philosophy department of Kyoto University, where Dr. Kitarō Nishida, who was also from Ishikawa Prefecture, was teaching.

I entered the university, but I no longer had any zeal for academic learning ... I idled away the three years of my university life without studying philosophy. And eventually the university people probably thought, "Since this fellow will not accomplish anything here, we had better get rid of him as soon as possible." Thus they let me graduate.

I had been reduced to being a hopelessly bad student—and it was solely because of listening to that three-day, or more accurately three-evening, lecture by Rev. Akegarasu when I was a sophomore in high school. After listening to his lecture, my life started to take a funny direction. Even now, as an extension of that, I am idling away my time. I am a carefree pleasure seeker, amusing myself by doing whatever I like.

For example, yesterday I went to a school in Nishi Minoa to study Buddhism with the schoolteachers there. All day, from 10:00 A.M. to 5:30 P.M., I just grumbled about whatever interested me. I gave them an idle and funny talk. I spent a thoroughly enjoyable time.

As I say this, you may ask me, "Then what made you become what you are now—a carefree pleasure seeker?" I think my answer to this question is as follows:

As I said earlier, I attended Rev. Akegarasu's lecture on the "Verses in Praise of a Buddha" when I was a sophomore in high school. On one summer evening, I listened to him for one and half hours. That lecture was the first of three evening lectures. I had never heard him speak before.

I paid one *yen* and fifty *sen* for admission to the city hall. They gave me the text of the "Verses in Praise of a Buddha." Then I sat on a thin mat on the wooden floor ... Since Rev. Akegarasu was almost blind at that time, he walked with a cane. He came up to the stage of the city hall to the sound of his stick hitting the floor. I was sitting almost in the center of the audience. I saw him settle into a chair on the stage; and I said to myself, "Oh, this is Rev. Akegarasu."

Rev. Akegarasu first looked over the whole audience in the hall. Since he had almost lost his eyesight at that time, he, I now think, probably was not able to see what people were doing. But he said, "Well, I see there, there, and there that some of you have brought pencils, notebooks, and paper. If you have, get out!" All the people there had paid an admission fee to listen to his lecture. I, for example, paid one *yen* and fifty *sen* for the three lectures. All of the audience had paid at least fifty *sen* for one lecture. Yet he told all those with a pen and paper to leave immediately.

Rev. Akegarasu said this before he started his lecture. At that time I was a high school student. It was my business to take notes on the teachers' lectures in class, and I was astounded by Rev. Akegarasu's words. Since I had not brought a pencil and paper with me, I breathed easy and told myself, "Well, I don't have to leave." At the same time I thought, "What an unreasonable thing he is saying!"

Nobody actually followed his words and left the place. He then said,

> If you don't want to leave, put your paper and pencils away! What on earth are you going to do with your notes? You may say that you will clarify some of the unclear points in my talk by reviewing your notes at home. But if you don't understand me now when I am talking directly to you, face to face, how could you understand me through your notes at home? So if you don't want to leave, please put your paper and pencils away.

Then, pointing to a place in his forehead, he said,

> If you don't have any place to focus your eyes, just look here! Just look at this part of my body! Just listen to whatever I say over the next three evenings! Then in these three evenings you will feel some kind of flash. That's good enough. Even if you don't remember at all when or how that flash came up, it's all right. If a flash hits you, that's good enough.

Rev. Akegarasu taught us that truth is a flash. I believe that this has something to do with the truth of impermanence.

Thus even before he got into the main topic, the *Larger Sukhāvatīvyūha-sūtra*, he had already, I now realize, talked about the

27

main topic of his lecture. I say this because the truth of impermanence is the only truth that Śākyamuni taught, and Rev. Akegarasu had already discussed it when he told the audience how to listen to him.

What kind of truth did Śākyamuni discover in this world? He discovered one truth, and he called it "impermanence." Impermanence is something you cannot grasp. If you can grasp a thing, it is no longer impermanent. The truth of impermanence is that all existing things are being transformed moment after moment—that things and our minds are changing moment after moment and do not stay the same for even a second. Thus if there is anything that is fixed, there cannot be any truth of impermanence. This truth can only be described as a flash.

People here in Nagano Prefecture really love fireworks. I am originally from Ishikawa Prefecture. But I have been living in Nagano for over twenty years, and I feel that nobody in Japan loves fireworks more than Nagano people. I think the real taste of a firework is that as soon as it appears, it disappears. So if a firework spreads in the dark sky and maintains the same shape for a long time, there is no taste of a firework. For example, think of a firework that looks like a chrysanthemum. As soon as the beautiful flower spreads in the sky, it disappears and the sky gets completely dark again. I think that is why fireworks are enjoyable.

A flash is something like a firework. As soon as it shines, it disappears. So Rev. Akegarasu was saying, "If you can say that a flash came to you because you heard such and such words, that kind of flash is a fixed concept and cannot be an authentic one." Thus I heard directly from him that truth is a flash. Pointing at his forehead, he taught us, "If you have a sharp flash of truth during the course of my talk, that's it. Then you have not wasted your time by attending my lectures for three evenings."

When I listened to those words, I felt as if everything I had cherished was completely taken away from me. As I said earlier, I was a student at that time. A student must remember the content of a teacher's lecture by diligently taking notes. He memorizes those notes and he writes down answers in exams. He relies upon what he has memorized. In this way he accumulates all kinds of knowledge. And this accumulated knowledge is called scholarship. As a student, my main concern up to that time was the accumulation of knowledge.

If truth is a flash as Rev. Akegarasu said, then scholarship could no longer exist in me. I think my academic studentship was terminated at that moment.

A couple of years before I listened to Rev. Akegarasu I entered high school from junior high school. I had been accustomed to studying hard in junior high school, so when I was a freshman in high school, some teachers were happy about me and said, "This year we've got an excellent student." Although I do not think I studied hard in high school, I received good grades, particularly in English and mathematics. But after my sophomore year, when I listened to Rev. Akegarasu, I suddenly became a strange student. Since I had heard that truth is a flash, all scholarship, which is based on memorized ideas, ceased to have any meaning for me. Nobody any longer called me an exemplary student or a genius.

Then, after graduating from high school, I entered a university and majored in philosophy. Since philosophy is also a kind of scholarship, how could I, who despised scholarship, study it? I really think it is strange that a bad student like myself was allowed to graduate from a university and receive a diploma.

It is somewhat embarrassing for me to tell the following to you schoolteachers, but when I was in the final year at my university, although I was supposed to be in Kyoto, I was not there. For six months I was not in Kyoto. Where did I go? I went to Shiono Misaki Point [a scenic seaport village located at the southern end of the island of Honshū] in Wakayama Prefecture. I heard later that the villagers there looked at me with pity and wondered, "Has this young student suffered a nervous breakdown, or a broken heart?" I was not suffering from either. For six months I was having a very good time there. From March on (March is part of winter there), I swam in the ocean. I loved swimming.

I was a student in my final year in the philosophy department of a university. I was supposed to finish up my studies by writing a dissertation and graduate with an excellent record. Completely ignoring my studies, I casually visited Shiono Misaki Point.

I rode a 1,200 ton steamer from Tempōsan Pier in Osaka to Kushimoto. I asked someone at an inn in Kushimoto if there was a place in Shiono Misaki Point where I could stay. He told me, "Many oil painters visit Shiono Misaki Point, and there are private homes where they usually stay. If you go there and ask someone, you'll find such a home." So I went there and sure enough, there were homes like that. I stayed in one of those homes for half a year. Every day I went out to the ocean and swam. Some of you may have visited the place and know there is a wide grass field right on Misaki Point. Behind that stretch of grass, there is a forest. Although it may have looked as if I were doing Zen in that forest, I was just sitting and thinking various things. I had fun with the young people of the fishing village.

How disappointing it was for my parents! They had hoped I would study diligently at the university, but I was playing around in Shiono Misaki Point. Since I could not survive in Shiono Misaki Point without money, my parents were kind enough to send me some money by registered mail. I have forgotten how many tens of *yen* it was. Every month I received this by registered mail and paid my room and board. What a carefree life it was!

Since that kind of life could not last forever, since I had to graduate from the university, I left Shiono Misaki Point after six months and returned to Kyoto. Then I satisfied the minimum requirements for graduation; I attended classes and submitted the necessary papers. But as I said earlier, the truth of the matter is that the university people had already given up on me; they felt that there was no use retaining me in the university and wanted to kick me out of the school. That was my graduation. Actually I was almost in the category of "repeater" or "dropout." So my graduation was more like an ejection from school. I am such a graduate from Kyoto University, so you schoolteachers cannot expect much from me.

All of this happened entirely because of Rev. Akegarasu, because of his talk. He was entirely responsible for all this. Even before he started to lecture on the "Verses in Praise of a Buddha," while he was telling us how to listen to him, I was completely killed by him. I really feel now that he had already finished his discussion of the main topic when he made those preliminary remarks, although he then started his lecture and went on for several hours over three evenings. What did I hear from him? I just heard that truth is a momentary flash. So I think you cannot gain anything beneficial by listening to such a person as myself.

After those words, Rev. Akegarasu started to lecture on the "Verses in Praise of a Buddha." We listened to him explain the verses one by one. His whole lecture was transcribed by someone and we can now see it in book form. But I am not moved at all by that book. The book is so different from what I experienced that evening. For example, the words which so deeply struck me cannot be found in that book, because they were Rev. Akegarasu's preliminary remarks, not part of his lecture on the text. But those words were the most important for me. My entire being, to the core of my bone marrow, was shaken by them.

When a lecturer opens a textbook and says, "Now let's begin with this passage ...," it is sometimes the case that you have already missed the most important part of his lecture. It sometimes happens that the lecturer touches upon a deep truth in his casual talk before his formal lecture. So I think that casual conversations are quite important.

I think it is really marvelous that Rev. Akegarasu talked about the most important thing in Buddhism before he started his lecture. He had already discussed the truth of impermanence. There is no Buddhism, no teaching of Śākyamuni, aside from the truth of impermanence.

In the Pāli language, impermanence is *anicca*. Pāli belongs to the family of Indo-European languages, like German and English. So by attaching the prefix *a* to some words, we can make antonyms. For example, in German, attaching *a* to *Theismus* (theism) forms the word *Atheismus* (atheism). Similarly in Pāli *a* is attached to *nicca* (permanence) and the word *anicca* (impermanence) is formed. Don't you think this word *nicca* has an interesting sound? *Nicca nicca* sounds like the Japanese word *necha necha* (sticky sticky). It sounds like something is firmly sticking, or strongly fixed. This *nicca*-ness (fixedness) is negated by *a* and the word *anicca* (impermanence) is formed. *Anicca* means that there is nothing permanent, that everything is constantly moving and changing.

Yesterday, as I mentioned, I was studying Buddhism with school-teachers at Nishi Minoa. In a discussion session, one female teacher said to me, "Teacher, you talk about impermanence. But if you say everything is impermanent, we cannot have any fixed basis for our lives. We will be confused as to the purpose of our lives." But if there is a basis for one's life, that is *nicca*. That is something which we can grasp, or attach to. If we allow the existence of *nicca*, something permanent, we are no longer talking about Buddhism.

Anicca means that there cannot be any basis, position, or viewpoint. Everything we cherish is totally negated. The truth of impermanence means that there is nothing that we can rely upon in this world.

So any human efforts to construct a system of thought, an "ism," or a theory are futile. Impermanence does not allow us to have any fixed opinion, thought, viewpoint, or position. All those things are totally annihilated. Śākyamuni, I believe, taught only this truth of impermanence.

Thus when I was eighteen, I listened to Rev. Akegarasu, and everything which I relied on was taken away. The entire direction of my life was turned around.

(2/8, 1966)

2

The Most Important Thing in My Life

People often talk about two different approaches in Buddhism, reliance on one's own abilities and reliance on a power beyond the self. Common sense usually says that Zen emphasizes reliance on one's own abilities. But if a religion is authentic, it must teach reliance on a power beyond the self. No true religion teaches reliance on the self's abilities. Dr. Kitarō Nishida, under whom I studied at university, says the same thing in his book on religious philosophy. In that sense, the Zen master Dōgen certainly talks about the concept of reliance on a power beyond the self. This evening, I wish to conclude my lecture series by discussing Dōgen's emphasis on that concept.

Dōgen wrote other books besides his main work, the *Shōbō-genzō* (Treasury of the Eye of the True Teaching). One of his earliest writings, composed not long after he came back from China, is the *Gakudō-yōjin-shū* (Things a Student Should Know). This text has a chapter entitled "The Need for a True Teacher in Learning." In it we read the following sentence:

> If you do not have a true teacher, you had better not study Buddhism.[1]

Dōgen says here that learning done without a true teacher, without his guidance, is totally meaningless—that such learning is worse than not studying at all. He says that one absolutely needs a true teacher in learning; there can be no true learning without a true teacher. When we read a sentence like this, which talks about this essential condition for learning, how can we say that the Zen master Dōgen teaches reliance on one's own abilities?

When he was a little over twenty, Dōgen, unable to find a teacher in Japan, went to China to study. He had to go there on an unreliable Japanese sailboat, risking his young life. Traveling to various places in China in search of the right teacher, he finally met the Zen master Ju-ching on Mt. T'ien-t'ung. At the beginning of "A Discussion of the Way (Bendō-wa)," the first volume of his ninety-five-volume Shōbō-genzō, he says,

> Finally, when I visited the Zen master Ju-ching on Mt. T'ien-t'ung, the most important thing in my life, my search for the way, had ended.[2]

Dōgen says that when he visited this person, the most important thing in his life, the search for the way, which he had undertaken at the risk of death, had ended. No other expression could better describe his joy at meeting a true teacher. He sharply says "had ended."

The expression "had ended" could also mean that Dōgen died as soon as he met this Zen master Ju-ching. Here I cannot help thinking of Dōgen, who was completely killed by Ju-ching. If Dōgen's life were to continue after that, it was no longer his life; it was the life of something beyond himself. The most important objective in his life was fulfilled. Dōgen, having attained his goal in life, was totally nullified before Ju-ching. How could we think that the Dōgen who says something like this is teaching reliance on one's own abilities? How could we regard his Zen as a school that teaches reliance on one's own abilities?

Last evening Mr. Lin from China stood here and gave his talk. In his talk he said, "Although I studied at Keiō University, I did not understand why I came to Japan to study until I met Rev. Akegarasu.

But ever since I finally met the Rev. Haya Akegarasu, I have felt that it is quite significant that I came from China to study in Japan. That is the only thing I want to say to you." If Dōgen were in Mr. Lin's shoes, he would use the thoroughgoing expression, "The most important thing in my life, my search for the way, had ended."

Today we had an informal discussion session from morning to afternoon. There all of you talked about your happiness at meeting Rev. Akegarasu. When I heard you express your sincere gratitude to him, I secretly thought that you were feeling the same thing that Dōgen felt when he said his words.

I am one of the newcomers to this summer retreat. I have only come here for the last several years. But it was more than twenty years ago that I saw Rev. Akegarasu for the first time. When I was a sophomore in Shikō High School, Rev. Akegarasu came to the Kanazawa city hall and gave three lectures on the *Larger Sukhāvatīvyūha-sūtra*. I was fortunate enough to listen to him at that time.

During my second lecture the other day, we recited a passage from the "True Marks of All Dharmas (*Shohō-jissō*)" volume of the *Shōbō-genzō*. There Dōgen depicts the atmosphere of an evening on Mt. T'ien-t'ung so beautifully that one could call the description an epic poem. While we were reciting it, I was reminiscing about the time I first met Rev. Akegarasu more than twenty years ago, when I was eighteen. Dōgen writes:

> On that evening, faint moonlight was dripping through the space between two multistoried buildings. Although a cuckoo was constantly cooing, it was a quiet evening.[3]

Dōgen reminisces about that evening with deep feeling. This passage made my memories gush up. It was also an evening in summer when I first heard my teacher at the Kanazawa city hall. All the windows of the hall were open, and the cool night air was coming through. Rev. Akegarasu was making a fiery speech; he was driving the essence of Mahāyāna Buddhism deep into my heart. Then the sound of a bamboo flute came from the forest at the back of the hall and reached us through the open windows. Rev. Akegarasu noticed the sound and said as he listened to it, "Can you hear the sound of that bamboo flute?"

Then he started to talk about the sound of the bamboo flute being part of his lecture. Even now I vividly remember what he said at that time. Later, his lectures on those three evenings were published as *Lectures on "Verses in Praise of a Buddha."* [4] His words about the sound of the flute are recorded there.

When I recited the passage in the "True Marks of All Dharmas," I remembered that night. As I look back on that experience over twenty years ago when I was a teenager, I feel that the greatest event in my life took place on that evening—the event that Dōgen describes by saying, "Finally, when I visited the Zen master Ju-ching on Mt. T'ien-t'ung, the most important thing in my life, my search for the way, had ended."

I was killed by my teacher on that evening. The word "kill" may sound too wild. But I feel that I was totally *embraced* by the immense heart of my teacher.

Since then I have passed through different places. Because that experience took place when I was a high school student, it was followed by years in a university, where I studied philosophy. After I graduated from the university, many years passed. But the time was not ripe for a personal visit with Rev. Akegarasu. In those years I was struggling to find the right direction. I studied various things. For example, I attempted to construct my own philosophical system. And I spent a considerable amount of time studying Marxism with my friends. Now I can say that those years were an interim period, a period in which I was lost. But that period of lostness came after I had already been completely embraced by the immense heart of Rev. Akegarasu. I was experiencing lostness within my teacher's heart. Thus it did not matter so much. It was only a few waves in a huge ocean. After the period of lostness, I quite naturally returned to Rev. Akegarasu.

When I read that passage from "True Marks of All Dharmas," I could not help remembering the evening when I, a sophomore in high school, first met Rev. Akegarasu. I am what I am today because of that meeting.

At the beginning of my talk I quoted the sentence "If you do not have a true teacher, you had better not study Buddhism." What, then, is a true teacher? Can I, on my part, tell whether a certain person is a true teacher or not? Can I, for example, select a true teacher from three candidates, Mr. A, Mr. B, and Mr. C? The truth of the matter is that I do not yet understand what is true. How, then, can I, who do not yet understand what is true, determine whether a certain teacher is true or not? It is a mistake typical of a person who thinks in terms of objective logic[5] to believe that he can choose a true teacher from several candidates by comparing and evaluating them.

Thus to use a simple expression, it is because of karmic conditions that one meets with a true teacher. The true teacher is a person who totally kills me. He cuts my being into two halves by swinging a sharp sword directly into my forehead. In other words, a teacher can be said to be true if my entire being is completely embraced by his heart. In this way the true teacher is identified not by my subjective evaluation, but by an objective fact—by karmic conditions. Hence I think that a true teacher is something given to us by a power beyond the self.

I truly feel that the *Shōbō-genzō* was written by a person who appreciates a power beyond the self.

(8/20, 1950)

3

Standing-Death

1

"Standing-death" (*tachi-ōjō*) means dying instantly while remaining in a standing posture. It is being reduced to nothingness on the spot. The *nembutsu*[1] is standing-death, because in experiencing the *nembutsu* we lose the base on which we depend. Once, my teacher personally taught this to me. I want to write about my memory of that experience.

It was in the summer of 1947 or 1948. Together with several dozen of my students, I went from Nagano to the Rev. Haya Akegarasu's temple to participate in the summer retreat there. It was at one of the afternoon meetings that my teacher asked me to speak. Sitting on a chair on the platform, with my hands on a table, I started to talk. My teacher, seated on my left on a tatami mat without a cushion, was listening to me. This was in the main building of the Myōtatsu-ji temple in Kita-yasuda. Seated under my nose were well over two hundred people, and they were listening to what I was saying. All those I had brought from Nagano were also listening.

I had been speaking for ten or fifteen minutes when my teacher started to attack me with questions. I do not remember at all, now, what I was talking about at the time. But my teacher's remarks cut deeply into my heart. I felt as if a sharp knife had been thrust into it. My superficial and arrogant ideas were pinned down by my teacher's eyes, the eyes of a Tathāgata [one who embodies truth]. The attack was quite obvious to everyone there because my teacher always used very simple and direct words. I did not know how to answer. I could not keep on going with the same tone. The crown sitting so proudly on my head was smashed to pieces by my teacher.

I did not know what to say. I could not go on sitting on the platform, but I could not leave because I was halfway into my talk. I felt that I was in a very difficult position. My eyes moved about restlessly, not knowing where to focus. But the audience was really there, and I could not turn my eyes from them. Then my eyes encountered the eyes of those I had brought from Nagano. Some of the eyes said to me regretfully, sympathetically, "Mr. Maida, teacher, you have said a dumb thing. You shouldn't have said anything like that." Some of the pretty girls, thinking their teacher was suffering from an unreasonable attack, turned their eyes to me with compassion and pity. That compassion from those I had been teaching in Nagano was the most unbearable thing for me. People from other prefectures must have thought that it served me right, that I deserved my teacher's criticism because I had been so impudent and arrogant up to that time. But my eyes never turned to those people. In the public eye, in front of those who loved me very much, I was humiliated.

I was so overwhelmed with shame that for the first time in my life, I wished the floor would open up and engulf me. I actually did look down at the tatami mat on my right (since my teacher was sitting on my left) and thought that if a hole were there, I would jump into it. There was no hole.

Totally deprived of my position in the presence of other people, I still had to go on talking—I didn't know what else to do. So, with a strange smile and a perplexed expression, I continued to talk for a while without knowing what I said.

It was not until I had talked for five or ten minutes more that my teacher began his second attack. As the proverb says, "If you kill a man, you cannot help seeing his blood"; he never allowed me any escape and pursued me ruthlessly. He didn't stop until he had totally wiped out my position. At that moment I thought, "What an ill-natured person he is, what a tough devil!" I complained to myself that he should have called me into his study privately if he had something to advise me about, instead of disgracing me in such a public place. Since I had no hope of finding a hole to hide in, I cried silently (though outwardly there were no tears). Feeling bitterly the futility and awkwardness of my being, I put a faltering end to my talk. When I got off the platform, I couldn't help but feel that the talk had been nothing but an inconsistent chain of mumblings.

In this way, my teacher totally deprived me of my position, left me standing where there was nothing but nothingness, and made me realize that I cannot find anything dependable in this world.

2

This was the greatest smashing of my being by the spiritual hammer of my teacher. I had never seen my teacher without getting sharp words from him that totally destroyed my position. But this was the first time I met this great devil face to face. In this experience I felt my teacher's very great compassion for me. What else could this have been but very great compassion? He taught me, very thoroughly, that there is nothing, not even one thing, that is dependable in this world. He personally took away my position so as to let me know this essential teaching and the truth of the *nembutsu*.

He could do this only by disgracing me in the public eye. If he had asked me to come to his study and there admonished me—as I had secretly hoped—I should not have known real shame. If he had done that, he could not have let me see the real self which I must be ashamed of. My own self would not have been annihilated.

Great compassion had only this means of making me see: depriving me of my disguise and disgracing me in front of the dear young ones from Nagano Prefecture who had always considered me their great teacher. The greatest compassion works as a sword of the devil. It works as a ruthless, thoroughly destructive force. It was at this very moment that my heart was abundantly filled with the great

40

compassion of the Tathāgata through my teacher. This is why I call my teacher "the teacher in my life." How can we define the working of the teacher if not as that which smashes the personality of his student away? The teacher is absolute negation. He is nothing but this. Encountering this absolute negation is meeting the true teacher in one's life. It gives us our greatest joy in life.

3

Rev. Akegarasu was crushed by the spiritual hammer of the Rev. Manshi Kiyozawa day after day, night after night, for three years while he was living in the Kōkō-dō dormitory in Tokyo. Never, not even once, did Rev. Kiyozawa express approval of Akegarasu's ideas. He never once agreed with him or admitted that what he was saying was right. Even when Akegarasu repeated an idea of Rev. Kiyozawa's—after realizing its truth—Rev. Kiyozawa would flatly contradict the idea, saying that it was no longer true. For this reason, Rev. Akegarasu had no place to stand. It went on like this until the very end of those three years.

Many young men left the Kōkō-dō dormitory because they would have nothing to do with a teacher like Rev. Kiyozawa who constantly contradicted all of their ideas. My teacher used to say smilingly that he stuck fast to Rev. Kiyozawa to the end. He also told me in reminiscence that his greatest happiness in being Rev. Kiyozawa's student was that he was able to learn the truth of the *nembutsu*, which is the truth of "no position." My teacher was keenly aware of the kindness of Rev. Kiyozawa in contradicting him and never allowing him to hold a position. There was continuous negation, no approval, to the end. This is what the true teacher is like. In life, the true teacher exists only in this way—there is no other way.

For Plato, Socrates must have been such a teacher. What else could Hōnen have been for Shinran during the three years when Shinran visited him at his meditation hall in Yoshimizu? We can easily imagine how Shinran was deluged by sharp verbal thrusts from Hōnen, who was well known for his wisdom. It was only through those thrusting, gouging words, day after day, night after night, that Shinran was obliterated. Shinran became Shinran in this way. Purely for this reason, Shinran revered Hōnen as the teacher in his life and as a historical appearance of the Tathāgata. If you imagine that Hōnen patted Shinran on the head, thinking him a promising youth, you are millions of miles away from the actual teacher-student relationship. The crushing and smashing of my head into pieces is an act accomplished entirely by a power beyond the self. I cannot do anything about my own head.

The real experience of a power beyond the self, the nothingness of our subjective self, can be given to us simply through meeting with a true spiritual guide. I think of my standing-death at Kita-yasuda. My appreciation of my teacher's great warmth is beyond measuring. He killed me on the spot. For me, supreme good fortune is nothing but this. In this term, standing-death, I hear a call, "Come immediately!"[2]

If someone asks me what I have learned from my teacher, I answer, standing-death. He taught me nothing else. What we have to learn from the teacher is only this one thing, this one word: standing-death. This is the only truth in Buddhism. My teacher taught me kindly, using tens of millions of words. But what shook me most, as the shortest and yet deepest truth, was this one thing. It was absolute negation. It is by no means an easy thing to meet with a true teacher. This is why Shinran said that entrusting oneself to the Buddha or Dharma is the most difficult thing one can do.

(7/31, 1966)

4

Nothingness

The Rev. Haya Akegarasu once criticized the religious views of scholars, saying, "Scholars study religion from books, but they are not actually crushed by a real human being. That is why they are no good. They are not thoroughgoing. Don't you think, Mr. Maida, that you and I are fortunate by comparison because we have met with real human beings?"

For Rev. Akegarasu the "real human being" was, of course, Rev. Kiyozawa. But whom did he mean when he said, "Mr. Maida, you are fortunate to have met a real human being"? My impression at that moment was that he was talking about himself. He had taken up the task of crushing me. I felt as if he were telling me, "Since I will crush you, you will be all right." I have never been able to forget the special feeling I had at that moment.

Yes, indeed. I consider it the most fortunate event of my life that Rev. Akegarasu kindly crushed me. My indescribably delightful feeling of liberation and freedom comes from that. Is there anything more delightful than meeting with a real human being? One cannot understand what I am speaking about if he has not met with a real human being and been completely crushed.

No matter how seriously one may read books or spend time in thought, one's deep-rooted self-attachment cannot fall out. So when I see someone who has not met with a real human being, I feel sorry for him. I really feel it to be my greatest good fortune that I was able to see my teacher, a real human being.

For me, my teacher was a real human being who kindly admonished me. He was nothing else. Sometimes I thought he was the greatest of all devils. I was terrified at having my weak spots pointed out so sharply. I was appalled to see the deepest parts of my mind, parts which I was not aware of, being discovered and revealed. I no longer had any place to stand in this world. The ground I was standing on started to collapse and I was completely buried. Everything in me was taken away from me. He kept kicking me down until I fell flat. It reminds me of the old man Shōju who kicked Hakuin [1685–1768, a Rinzai Zen master] off the cliff near his Shōju-an hermitage in Iiyama. This was my teacher. This is the core of my memory of him.

Did Rev. Akegarasu consider me his student? No. He once introduced me to his congregation as a student of Dr. Kitarō Nishida in Kyoto. Although Rev. Akegarasu admonished me, he did so without the idea that I was his student. He always treated me as a human being, as his equal. It was in this man-to-man relationship that he crushed me, and crushed me with the totality of his being.

Do I consider myself a student of Rev. Akegarasu? The answer to this question is also no. Ours was not the fixed relationship of teacher and student. If I consider myself Rev. Akegarasu's student, then "I, the student" will still be there. There is not even such an "I." I am *nothing* before him. I am not even his student. There is nothing. This is my honest feeling. So I think it rather strange when people call me a student of Rev. Akegarasu. In the relationship between teacher and student, the Dharma is supposed to be transmitted from teacher to student. There is no Dharma to be transmitted from him to me. There is nothing. I am simply nothing before my teacher.

Some people talk about the transmission of the Dharma. I consider them leisurely people. For a person whose entire self is crushed by his teacher, what could remain? Not even the Dharma. There remains only *the fact* that one's self was completely crushed. That is why I say that my teacher liberated me completely.

I am most grateful that Rev. Akegarasu gave me absolute freedom. I am not obligated to him in any way. There is not even one thing that I must do because I am his student. If I am myself, that's good enough. What else could I be besides myself? I have not received any Dharma from my teacher to transmit to others. I just live as myself. The teacher has a poem:

> There is no "my Dharma" to be transmitted.
> There is no "my student," either.
> There are only the stars twinkling in the high sky.[1]

(9/7, 1954)

45

5

Rev. Akegarasu and Rev. Kiyozawa

1

The Rev. Haya Akegarasu said, "During the three years that I lived with my teacher the Rev. Manshi Kiyozawa at the Kōkō-dō dormitory in Tokyo, he never once accepted anything I said." Suppose that one day Rev. Akegarasu asserted something; his logic was then completely refuted by Rev. Kiyozawa and he recognized the correctness of Rev. Kiyozawa's logic. The next day Rev. Akegarasu would agree with what Rev. Kiyozawa said the day before; but when Rev. Akegarasu echoed him, Rev. Kiyozawa completely destroyed that, too. The following day, after trying to figure out what Rev. Kiyozawa meant, Rev. Akegarasu made another assertion; and again Rev. Kiyozawa crushed him completely.

Rev. Kiyozawa never let Rev. Akegarasu grab at any definite conclusion; and what is more, he never hung onto such conclusions himself, either. He had nothing to rely on, nothing to dwell in, and nothing to possess. Rev. Akegarasu constantly received strong negation from his teacher for the last three years of his teacher's life. Rev. Akegarasu said, "During those three years he thoroughly crushed me." It was a teacher-student relationship in which the teacher never once said to the student, "You are right."

It is traditional in Zen that the Zen master finally affirms the enlightenment of his student [by giving him a robe and an iron begging bowl]. Such an affirmation is so lukewarm when compared with what Rev. Kiyozawa did! One who certifies the student's enlightenment is not a true teacher. There is no way of putting a stamp of approval on the truth of nothingness [or impermanence]. To certify is itself already a fixed action.

As far as I am concerned, Rev. Akegarasu never once affirmed my enlightenment. He did not even consider me his student. Whenever he introduced me to others, he said, "This is a student of Dr. Nishida of Kyoto University." As a matter of fact, he did not have even one student. In a poem composed in his later years, he said,

> I have no teacher to learn from.
> I have no students to teach.
> I have nothing,
> There are only the stars twinkling in the high sky.[1]

After I moved to Nagano Prefecture, he scolded me in this way: "Since you moved to Nagano, no one makes you feel ignorant. All these little kids call you teacher there. So you have already become a teacher, have you?"

When I was editing *Great Assembly* (*Kōdaiye*), Rev. Akegarasu's personal journal, I told a group of people who came to the teacher's retreat that since I wanted to get more subscribers, I would like to publicize the magazine among the labor unions, for example. And my teacher practically knocked me over by telling me, "What are you saying? Those who want to wave the red flag—let them enjoy it. You are acting like you have already attained Enlightenment."

Once, during Shinran's Memorial Week at his temple, Rev. Akegarasu asked me to give a talk to a group of people who had gathered in the main hall. Almost all of the audience were old women, farmers' wives. They wore peasant scarves over their heads, had runny noses, and kept sniffling and snuffling as I talked. I gave a philosophical talk on a subject that I myself was struggling with at the time. My teacher listened to me with the old women. When I had finished, he started to go back to his room. Gently pushing aside the old women who crowded around him, he told them, "Mr. Maida studied philosophy—a very difficult subject—at the university. So he has to unburden himself to other people to feel satisfied. You ladies and I are fortunate because we are liberated by the *nembutsu* alone." They listened to what my teacher said, and they did not laugh. It was impressive to me that they were very quiet.

Thus Rev. Akegarasu treated me always. He never said, "You are right." He never let me stay in one place. Between my teacher and me there was only nothingness. Only nothingness appeared there. He never saw any importance in me. Furthermore, he never saw any importance in himself, either. I was less important to him than the farmers' wives who were chanting the *nembutsu* with their noses running. I, a man who was caught up in the logic of philosophy, was totally without significance to him.

Because he was like this, I could be without any reserve around him. I could say to my teacher anything that I wanted to. There was always an atmosphere like a spring breeze between us. In front of him I was never expected to be anything. I was meeting a teacher who was nothingness. If he had seen some importance in me, then there would have been a limited existent teacher who saw some importance in me. But that was not the case at all. So I could behave as freely as I wanted.

In this way my teacher absolutely liberated me. This is how I learned the teaching of liberation. By completely crushing me, by even ignoring me, he liberated me. To me my teacher was nothingness. Thus I have touched his absoluteness.

2

As Rev. Kiyozawa completely crushed Rev. Akegarasu, so Hōnen crushed Shinran until there was nothing left. Because of "no affirmation," Shinran respected Hōnen as his teacher. If any teacher affirms his student, then their relationship becomes a relative relationship of man to man. Then Hōnen's absoluteness could not have been manifested. For instance, the sun has no intention of illuminating me; the sun simply goes its own way, shining in the middle of the sky. This is how Shinran saw Hōnen. This is how Rev. Akegarasu saw Rev. Kiyozawa and how I see my teacher.

During the three years with Rev. Kiyozawa at the Kōkō-dō dormitory, Rev. Akegarasu surely came to embody the *nembutsu,* the truth that there is nothing in the world that one can rely on, dwell in, or possess. He became himself. Thus the nothingness of Buddhism became my teacher. More accurately, the Rev. Akegarasu who lived absolute nothingness was born there. What I have so far discussed seems to be the most important key to understanding the essence of his being.

I would like to comment further on Rev. Akegarasu's free relationship with Rev. Kiyozawa. While I was editing his *Great Assembly,* he told me, "You may change my articles any way you like. I used to revise Rev. Kiyozawa's articles for *Spiritual World* (*Seishin-kai*) freely. I'll feel bad if you don't do the same thing without reservation."

While we were talking, he received a visit from Mr. Kunizō Nakata, formerly the head of the Ishikawa Prefectural Library and at this time connected with the University of Tokyo Library. Mr. Nakata said, "I've just visited Dr. Kitarō Nishida's Memorial Hall in the town of Unoke in Kawakita County. His articles are being displayed there. I am so grateful because I was fortunate enough to be able to touch Dr. Nishida's manuscript articles with my own hands!"

Hearing this, Rev. Akegarasu snorted, "Huh! What are you so grateful about? We used to blow our noses on Rev. Kiyozawa's old manuscript pages and then throw them away." I thought to myself, "No question about that, because Rev. Akegarasu regards even his own articles as waste material once they have come out of him."

I also recall other things about Rev. Akegarasu. In one summer retreat at his temple he gave a seven-day series of talks on Rev. Kiyozawa's article "The Great Path of Absolute Power Beyond the Self"—an article consisting of passages that Rev. Kanae Tada selected from Rev. Kiyozawa's *December Fan Diary* (*Rōsen Nikki*[2]) and edited. In the final section of the article Rev. Kiyozawa talks about the material aspect of life. He first says, "An independent person should stand always on the precipice between life and death." Then he says,

A person who is prepared for death can enjoy whatever food or clothing he happens to have. He can calmly accept death if food and clothing should be exhausted. If he has family and relatives, he should see to their welfare before his own, taking for himself only what remains.[3]

With regard to this, Rev. Akegarasu said, "Rev. Kiyozawa had tuberculosis, and in addition he was a selfish man. So instead of feeding his wife and children first, he always had the first and best of everything. I saw it with my own eyes." Rev. Akegarasu described his teacher as he was. There was no "genuine trust" for Rev. Akegarasu aside from seeing his teacher as he was.

When Rev. Kiyozawa passed away, all his students came up with the same idea for his Dharma name: "Power of Genuine Trust (*Shinriki-in*)." Thus Rev. Kiyozawa unconditionally trusted not only his disciples but also everyone. Because he trusted Rev. Akegarasu completely, he crushed him completely, until there was nothing left. Because he wanted to make Rev. Akegarasu become himself and become independent, because he trusted him to become himself and become independent, he crushed him.

I have earlier used the word nothingness to describe Rev. Kiyozawa. Now I will use another term, genuine trust, to describe him. He is indeed the Power of Genuine Trust. Rev. Akegarasu's genuine trust was directly transmitted to him from Rev. Kiyozawa.

What Rev. Akegarasu says about his teacher—that instead of feeding his wife and children, he ate delicious food first—vividly shows that he had absolute, genuine trust in his teacher. When he says so, he and his teacher are completely one, as [foolish] ordinary persons.[4]

3

The Zen master Bankei [1619–90] talked about "no-arising." He declared,

If things do not arise, naturally they do not perish. So it is superfluous to talk about both no-arising and no-perishing. For me, only no-arising is good enough.[5]

This is the so-called No-Arising Zen of Bankei.

Arising presupposes something from which something arises. It refers to a transition from one phase to another. Thus when there is arising there is always a relative relationship between two phases. When we recognize a thing as it is without paying attention to its relative relationship [with its past state], there is no arising. No-arising is an absolute recognition of things. In no-arising two questions cease: "What has turned into this?" and "What will this turn into?"

For instance, in talking about my life, I do not have to regret my past mistakes; I do not have to hope for future achievements. I do not have to rely on my past career. I do not have to fear the future. I have only the present moment. The only thing for me to do is to live the present moment wholeheartedly. *No, the only thing there is* is my own shining life. The same thing can be said about others. We do not have to blame them for their past mistakes. We do not have to expect anything of their future.

No-arising means that a thing exists as it is—as the self-determination of absolute nothingness.[6] Thus a thing does not perish, either. We do not have to become attached to nothingness by emphasizing perishing [or extinction]. No-perishing means that a thing exists as it is.

No-arising is genuine emptiness [a perspective from which things are seen as having no permanent existence], and no-perishing is wonderful existence [a perspective from which things are seen as manifesting the flow of life, or the truth of impermanence]. No-arising is expressed in the phrase, Form is emptiness.[7] No-perishing is expressed in the phrase, Emptiness is form. Neither arising nor perishing means that a thing exists as it is. It means that a person is a [foolish] ordinary person. It means flat-ordinariness [the truth that things are all right as they are].[8] It is on this basis that Rev. Kiyozawa and Rev. Akegarasu met. They were [foolish] ordinary persons. Rev. Kiyozawa was a [foolish] ordinary person who ate delicious food before he gave his family any. Rev. Akegarasu was a [foolish] ordinary person who arbitrarily changed even his teacher's writings when they did not satisfy him and who blew his nose on his teacher's manuscripts. There was neither a teacher nor a student. There was only nothingness. This was a relationship based on absolute genuine trust.

Nothingness, genuine trust, and neither-arising-nor-perishing are all synonyms. Both Rev. Kiyozawa and my teacher simply lived a life of neither arising nor perishing. My teacher was enabled to embody nothingness by Rev. Kiyozawa. For several decades after that, he lived a life of the utmost freedom, just being a [foolish] ordinary person. There is no Buddhism aside from living one's life freely as nothingness. Rev. Akegarasu lived his life as a real disciple of the Buddha.

Although I have used the expression "living one's life freely as nothingness," nothingness alone is enough description, because freedom inevitably comes out of this nothingness. This is similar to Bankei's view that no-arising is good enough and no-perishing is unnecessary.

Here nothingness is subjective nothingness. It is selflessness. It means not considering oneself important. It means not thinking that such and such actions are good or such and such actions are bad on the basis of one's infatuated view of the self. There is nothing spectacular about human beings. They cannot do anything remarkably good or evil with their five- or six-foot bodies, even if they try hard. That is why Shinran declared:

> Don't fear even evil! For there is no evil strong enough to impede the Innermost Aspiration [or Vow] of Amida Buddha.
>
> (*Tannishō*, Chapter 1)

Rev. Akegarasu subjectively understood this nothingness. That is, he understood that in Shinran's teaching, this nothingness refers to selflessness. This nothingness of Shinran was driven into Rev. Akegarasu through the living personality of Rev. Kiyozawa. Shinran, by assuming the form of Rev. Kiyozawa, could not help but make Rev. Akegarasu embody selflessness.

The same thing can be said about me. Shinran, by assuming the form of Rev. Akegarasu, must have appeared in front of me.

Rev. Kiyozawa was not attached to the *Kyōgyōshinshō* (Teaching, Practice, Genuine Trust, and Attainment[9]) at any time during his short life. My teacher was the same way; he lived his life by the *Tannishō*

(Notes Lamenting the Differences[10]) alone. This emphasis on the *Tannishō* was directly transmitted to him by Rev. Kiyozawa.

See if Rev. Kiyozawa ever used even one Buddhist technical term in his articles in *Spiritual World*, starting from his article entitled "Spiritual Awareness,"[11] which was placed at the beginning of the first issue of the journal. He wrote in the modern, everyday language of the Meiji period [1868–1911], language which was familiar to people. It was quite natural that my teacher, who had Rev. Kiyozawa as his teacher, wrote only to talk openly about himself.

Pay close attention to the fact that Shinran always treated his *Kyōgyōshinshō* as personal throughout his life and that he did not let anyone except a few disciples see it. He never intended to force it on others. It was a text only for himself. It was, as it were, a private and secret text. But posterity has brought it out and has been forcing it on others. How many people are there in the world who have seen the *Kyōgyōshinshō*, become attached to it, and lost their freedom! The *Tannishō* symbolizes liberation from this type of attachment to the *Kyōgyōshinshō*.

4

Late in his life, Rev. Akegarasu started writing "Some Thoughts on the *Kyōgyōshinshō*." In it he expressed his desire that the *Kyōgyōshinshō* be translated into the seven major languages of the world and spread among all people. To help realize this wish of my teacher, I have made public the *Bandō-bon* version of the *Kyōgyōshinshō*;[12] for I considered it indispensable that we have a reliable base text for the translation.

At one time while I was editing my teacher's *Great Assembly* journal, I moved my teacher's "Some Thoughts on the *Kyōgyōshinshō*" from the beginning of the journal, where it was supposed to be placed, to the end. Then I received a scolding from him. He wrote an article entitled, "A Complaint to Mr. Maida about the Editing of *Great Assembly*."[13] I can say that I have responded to this scolding from my teacher with my recent publication of the *Bandō-bon* version.

I have said above that the *Kyōgyōshinshō* was a private and, further, secret book for Shinran. With this I associate the December Fan Hall, which my teacher's students built for him to celebrate his seventy-seventh birthday. This hall [which contains two statues: Rev. Kiyozawa's sitting statue and Rev. Akegarasu's statue of him worshipping Rev. Kiyozawa] appears to me to be an expression of a hidden hall inside my teacher's mind. It describes something in the very depths of his mind. That is, it is not a place where we should open the door and look in. I associate it with the Kannon [or Avalokiteśvara] statue that had been hidden for several centuries in the Hōryu-ji temple's Yumedono Hall, of which the December Fan Hall is a replica. It was not until the Meiji period that Ernest Fenollosa [1853–1908, a philosopher and art historian] came to Japan and forcibly removed the long white cotton cloth that had wrapped and concealed the Kannon statue. After that, people have gone to see the statue only as a work of art. Fenollosa had only an artistic interest in it.

We do not need to visit the December Fan Hall and see those two statues, of Rev. Kiyozawa and of my teacher worshipping him. It is more religious to think of the deep mind of Rev. Akegarasu which is hidden behind the closed doors.

Even now we have hidden Buddha statues. Nobody has ever seen the statue of Amida Buddha accompanied by his two Bodhisattvas that is kept in the Zenkō-ji temple. Thus some people even claim that the temple actually does not have such a statue! But every year several million men and women come to pay homage to this "nothingness." Since a Buddha embodies nothingness, this is most appropriate. Even if the Buddha statue, a small image that is said to have once been thrown into a moat in Naniwa Province, does exist in the temple, I somehow cannot picture those people gazing at it.

Are we supposed to visit the December Fan Hall and worship the statue of Rev. Kiyozawa in the center of it, considering him our Buddha? No! Rev. Kiyozawa was a reappearance of the Buddha only for Rev. Akegarasu. What we should think of here is the mind of Rev. Akegarasu who is worshipping his teacher.

That is why I have indicated that we should consider the Hall to be the Secret Hall, comparing it to the hidden Buddha at the Zenkō-ji temple. Even during the Statue Exhibition festival at that temple, they just show an imitation statue, not the real statue. Similarly, the only thing we should recognize in our December Fan Hall is nothingness— the *fact* that Rev. Akegarasu was killed with one sharp stroke of Rev. Kiyozawa's spiritual sword.

For Akegarasu, who was totally negated by Kiyozawa, there was not even Kiyozawa. Akegarasu worshipped only himself. He declared, "My denomination is the Akegarasu School. The only follower is myself. There is no need whatsoever to spread it." He powerfully shouted, "In the heavens and on the earth *my aloneness* is noble."[14] Rev. Akegarasu lived his life all by himself. Here the very teaching of Rev. Kiyozawa is alive—the teaching, "Never preach even if you die!" Since he really lived this teaching, he talked about the Akegarasu School and declared, "In the heavens and on the earth *my aloneness* is noble." Although the traditional way of reading *ten-jō ten-ga yui ga doku son* is "In the heavens and on the earth *I, alone, am* noble," he read the italicized part as "my aloneness is." He did not say he was noble by comparison with others. He is clearly talking about aloneness.

Rev. Akegarasu inscribed these eight characters [*ten ... son*] powerfully in large characters. We can see them in a frame, twelve feet wide and three feet high, on the wall of the Myōtatsu-ji temple. I consider them his masterpiece. This aloneness is synonymous with nothingness. If one does not exist as the self-determination of absolute nothingness, one is not alone. That is, acting as nothingness is called being alone. This was the only thing that Rev. Akegarasu attained under the guidance of Rev. Kiyozawa.

5

Through his association with Rev. Kiyozawa, Rev. Akegarasu was purified. The original and shining Akegarasu was revealed by Kiyozawa. The expression "instantly be what you really are"[15] refers to this. If Kiyozawa had not existed, Akegarasu would not have existed. If Hōnen had not existed, Shinran would not have appeared in this world. We who have met Rev. Akegarasu cannot appreciate Rev. Kiyozawa too highly for bringing him into this world.

"What one really is" refers to a real human being. In Rev. Akegarasu we have met a real human being. This real human being tasted both purity and impurity. He was not a so-called saint. He was a [foolish] ordinary person. It is by meeting with this [foolish] ordinary person that we have been liberated. The Rev. Akegarasu whom I met face to face—what could he have been except a [foolish] ordinary person? He exposed the very deep pit of desire and suffering that he knew as a [foolish] ordinary person. How clearly he showed us the desire and suffering deep in ourselves that we do not recognize! It was Rev. Akegarasu who made us know how bottomless our desire and suffering are.

In this real human being I have met the Buddha, Śākyamuni. For me the concrete image of Śākyamuni is nothing but the person of Akegarasu. I think Śākyamuni was a person entirely like Rev. Akegarasu. For example, my teacher was a humorous person. Śākyamuni must have been a humorous person also. And my teacher spoke easy, simple, and direct words. Śākyamuni was the same way; in him there was not even one thing that was ambiguous or difficult. Furthermore, my teacher was a cheerful person. Śākyamuni, who attained complete liberation from attachment to the self, could not have been other than cheerful.

Rev. Kiyozawa's final letter was addressed to Rev. Akegarasu. At the end of the letter he wrote, "Now it's time for this ghost to disappear."[16] His pseudonym December Fan is also humorous. Rev. Akegarasu used the pseudonym No Nothingness (*Bimu*), since its sound was a pun on his name Bin [which is an alternate pronunciation of his name Haya].

There were so many humorous episodes involving my teacher that I cannot enumerate them all. So let me put down only one of them.

When Mr. T., one of Rev. Akegarasu's students, was studying at Ōtani University, his wife had morning sickness. She could not sleep at night without Mr. T. stroking her abdomen. Then even when she got over her morning sickness, she had become addicted to his stroking her abdomen and could not go to sleep without it. Somehow this story reached Rev. Akegarasu's ears. When I visited him in his study, he laughingly related it. When someone visited him after me, he repeated the same story to him. In this way he repeated it to people one after the other. On that day he enjoyed talking about it all day long and did not get tired of it. But by the next day he had forgotten all about it.

It is by this Rev. Akegarasu that I am liberated. Complete freedom without attachment to the self is something of that sort. It is by this Akegarasu who speaks so unpretentiously about an erotic incident that I am liberated into a carefree and unrestrained world, into the world of the [foolish] ordinary person.

In Rev. Akegarasu's books of the *Kōsō-Sōsho* series,[17] how often we find his confessions to being a [foolish] ordinary person! Who else could have described and exposed his human nature in such an open manner? Rev. Akegarasu's appearance was not one bit grave, serious, or formal. He did not wear the mask of a teacher, or any other mask. He met us as a real [foolish] ordinary person. He did not have the smell of Buddhism, or the smell of ethics. He was what he was. He was what a real human being is. He was a real human being himself. This was liberation and freedom. Aside from this, where else could we find liberation of our total being?

In this very humor of my teacher, I saw the vivid and lively working of my teacher's Buddha-Dharma. It is a kind of humor that eradicates reliance on one's own abilities.

How many humorous episodes there were between my teacher and Rev. Kiyozawa! For example, Dr. Enryō Inouye[18] wanted to inquire about Buddhism and asked for an interview with Rev. Kiyozawa. Rev. Kiyozawa responded by saying, "Since I cannot go because it is inconvenient, I will send a young man to take my place." He wrote a letter saying, "Please listen to whatever this person says as my words." He handed the letter to Akegarasu and sent him to Dr. Inouye. He ignored scholars like Dr. Inouye. He asked Rev. Akegarasu to treat Dr. Inouye in whatever way he wanted. Here I see Rev. Kiyozawa's humor. Here I sense his words, "How could scholars understand Buddhism?"

Once when Dr. Shōson Miyamoto [a famous Buddhist scholar] greeted Rev. Akegarasu, he instantly replied, "You scholars are really unsavable!" In this incident I see the same humor.

No matter how seriously words are uttered by human beings, there is nothing significant in them. It was on this basis that Rev. Akegarasu spoke. He really hated advocating his own ideas and giving wordy explanations. He said whatever he wanted to, freely, without any reserve, without any attachment. Whenever I spoke, I talked about the subject as if I were handling it with sticky hands. Then my teacher used to say, "Since you are a teacher at a teachers' college, you are quite verbose." He also said, "I am quick and direct, as my name Haya (quick) indicates." My teacher also remarked that the Buddha-Dharma is like the flowing of water in a shallow stream. As a matter of fact, my teacher's Buddha-Dharma is perfectly summarized in that one remark.

Rev. Akegarasu is always whispering in my ear, "There is nothing to worry about. You had better do whatever you want to do." This is the Buddha-Dharma that I heard from him. This must be the Buddha-Dharma that he heard from Rev. Kiyozawa, who called himself December Fan—that is, good for nothing in this world. How comical it must have been to these two to see people describing the Buddha-Dharma as such and such, becoming attached to it, and sticking to it! They could not suppress their laughter. The Buddhism preached by Buddhist ministers and the Buddhism discussed by scholars will both be blown away by the laughter of these two teachers. Most concretely, the Buddha-Dharma is their humor itself.

In this way Rev. Akegarasu freely enhanced the Buddha-Dharma. He seems to have had a personality unprecedented in the Buddhist history of Japan.

Only nothingness. Only a [foolish] ordinary person. Only flat-ordinariness. As the Zen master Lin-chi [?–867] said, "Everything is ordinary and nothing is special."[19] When we truly understand this, there is neither a Rev. Akegarasu nor a Rev. Kiyozawa. There is only the world of the *nembutsu*, a world in which there is nothing that can be relied upon, dwelled upon, or possessed by us.

Throughout the past three periods (Meiji, Taishō, and Shōwa) in Japan, only Rev. Akegarasu has played this exquisite music [of the Dharma]. Five hundred or a thousand years from now, people in Japan and in the world will look up to Rev. Akegarasu as one of the brightest stars shining in Japanese Buddhist history. Together with Śākyamuni, Rev. Akegarasu will be looking down on this world with a smile.

I was able to see Rev. Akegarasu. For me, there is no Buddha-Dharma apart from him. He is the Buddha-Dharma. He is Śākyamuni himself. If this idea is a mistake, then all of my life has been a mistake. It is, however, all right. I could die with satisfaction.

(12/30, 1966)

6

The December Fan Hall

Q. I have heard that the Rev. Haya Akegarasu built a hall called the December Fan Hall. Is this true?

A. Yes, it is true. He built it on the grounds of his temple. It is patterned after the Yumedono Hall of the Hōryū-ji temple.

Q. What is enshrined there?

A. On a platform in the center of the hall, there is a sitting statue of the Rev. Manshi Kiyozawa, Rev. Akegarasu's teacher. And on the floor, there is a sitting statue of Rev. Akegarasu with his hands together, worshipping his teacher. That's all there is in the hall.

Q. What, then, do these statues mean?

A. With these two statues Rev. Akegarasu is saying, "I will worship my teacher forever. There is no other purpose to my life."

Q. Is it, then, something like a secret room where deep internal communion between teacher and student takes place?

A.   Yes, you can say that. Rev. Akegarasu is single-mindedly looking at Rev. Kiyozawa face to face. He is showing what an independent person is like, a person who does not pay any attention to other people.

Q.   Is there any precedent for this?

A.   I don't know if there have been other statues like this, but there is a spiritual precedent.

Q.   What's that?

A.   In the sixth chapter of the *Tannishō*, Shinran says, "I, Shinran, do not have even a single disciple."[1] If we were to describe the spirit of that hall in one sentence, that sentence of Shinran would be it.

Q.   What, then, is the ultimate teaching revealed in this sentence?

A.   It is the teaching: "Go the way of an independent person. Do so alone."

Q.   But there are two people in the hall, the teacher and student. Why do you say "alone"?

A.   That's the most important and difficult point. When the student kneels before the teacher, throwing down his entire life before him, the student no longer has his own life. There is only the life of the universe, a life in which his life is completely merged with the life of the teacher. If the student starts to live this *selfless life*, we can say that he is, for the first time, going the way of an independent person, alone.

Q.   Then Rev. Akegarasu is not idolizing Rev. Kiyozawa as a great master, is he?

A.   Of course not. To use a strong expression, even Rev. Kiyozawa is no longer there. There is only the shout of Rev. Akegarasu: "In the heavens and on the earth, my aloneness is noble."[2] If we cannot hear this shout, it's useless to visit that hall.

61

Q. Do you mean that there is twoness and oneness at the same time?

A. Yes. People must learn oneness there. But they tend to see only twoness. As a consequence of this, they make the mistake of idolizing Rev. Akegarasu, of becoming attached to him.

Q. Is that the so-called inappropriate reliance on a teacher?

A. Yes. People don't see the absolute in the teacher; they just see a relative human being. Although they claim to see the absolute through the teacher, they are actually committing the mistake of becoming attached to the human being. That's how people are trapped by the new religions [which mushroomed in Japan after World War II].

Q. Then if the hall enshrined a Buddha statue in the sanctuary as the main object of worship, that would prevent people from misunderstanding the intent of Rev. Akegarasu, wouldn't it?

A. But since Rev. Akegarasu believed that we are not making such a mistake, he placed only those two statues in the hall. So if we are careful and do not make such a mistake, we don't have to have another statue.

Q. It's indeed very difficult to appreciate the absolute, not a human being, isn't it?

A. Yes. The teaching that the hall is teaching us is not an easy one.

7

Be Yourself!

1. The Teacher's Teaching

If I were asked what I have learned from Rev. Akegarasu, I would answer, "I have just received the teaching—'You should be yourself!'"

Now I am going south, down to the Ina Valley ... so that I may be myself. I am not Rev. Akegarasu. I am nobody else. I am I. Thus I go my own way.

Going the way of a human being, I am attempting to taste thoroughly the highest joy and the deepest sorrow that can be experienced by a human being. I am attempting to live my life to the fullest. I am trying to be faithful to my own life as much as possible. I am trying to dig into the depths of my life.

Sometimes, when I am overwhelmed by a dazzling experience, I find myself inadvertently comparing myself with the teacher. I find myself intending to imitate him. But when I do that, I am forgetting my own life. I am not fully established in myself.

Then I feel the need to go back to myself and resume self-examination. I try to dig into my being and recover my own life. I hear a voice saying, "Resolutely transcend the teacher! Don't be attached to him!"

An absolutely unique human being in the heavens and on the
earth.
Am I not such a being?
Nowhere among my predecessors can I find
The model path that I should follow.

No matter how reckless it may appear,
No matter how hopeless it may appear,
I am going to explore the path
That nobody has ever trodden
In the history of the universe.
This is the path of absolute brightness,
Which stretches through absolute darkness.

The teacher solemnly tells me, "Go!"
As if sending me to the jaws of death,
He shouts at me, "Go your own way!"

(10/5, 1949)

2. *Élan Vital*

T'ieh-tsu Chüeh, a Zen student, visited Fa-yen, a Zen master.
Fa-yen asked T'ieh-tsu Chüeh, "Where are you from?"

T'ieh-tsu Chüeh answered, "I am from Chao-chou Province"
[which means "I am a student of the Zen master Chao-chou"].

Fa-yen said, "I have heard that the Zen master Chao-chou talks
about an oak tree. Is this true?"

T'ieh-tsu Chüeh answered, "No."

Fa-yen said, "These days everybody is saying that when a
monk asked Chao-chou, 'What was Bodhidharma's intention in
coming to China?,'[1] Chao-chou answered, 'That's an oak tree in
the garden.' Why do you say Chao-chou did not say it?"

T'ieh-tsu Chüeh answered, "*My teacher certainly does not say
such words.* I hope you do not slander him."

Fa-yen said, "This fellow T'ieh-tsu Chüeh is a real son of a
lion [an awakened one]."[2]

(Emphasis by Maida)

T'ieh-tsu Chüeh, a direct student of Chao-chou, must have known
of Chao-chou's words about the oak tree. But he told Fa-yen that

Chao-chou did not say such words. The Zen expression "My teacher does not say such words" derives from this story.

In a true teacher-student relationship, the student is not allowed to imitate his teacher; the teacher cannot be used for the student's self-enhancement. A person who is not Chao-chou cannot preach a sermon pretending to be Chao-chou. T'ieh-tsu Chüeh is standing there trampling his teacher under his feet. He is there all by himself. He is independent. There is no trace of Chao-chou.

We often say, "That person said such and such, and this person said such and such." But in the second chapter of the *Tannishō*, Shinran declares, "As far as I, Shinran, am concerned ..."[3]

Truth is always expressed in an individual, introspective, and subjective manner. We may call it the foremost point of "the vital force of life" (*élan vital*).[4]

As for myself, am I not complacently relying upon the Rev. Haya Akegarasu in saying, "Rev. Akegarasu said this and that"? The expression "My teacher does not say such words" is a blow that smashes my complacency. Life itself, or truth itself, is asking me, "All right, that's what Rev. Akegarasu said. What, then, are your words? What is the one phrase, or word, which describes your life?"

When T'ieh-tsu Chüeh said that his teacher did not say such words, T'ieh-tsu Chüeh himself was standing there as an oak tree. It is by this type of subjective transition—the transition from the teacher's position to that of the self—that religious truth can be grasped. Religious truth always tells us, "Stand by yourself!" Thus the shout "I am I" is the so-called lion's roar [the Buddha's roar]. Religion enables us to utter the lion's roar.

(10/14, 1957)

3. Foreword of the First Issue of the Journal *Kōsō*

Rev. Akegarasu has passed away. He is no longer in this world. No matter how desperately we may call him, he does not answer with the voice that can be heard by our ears.

So we, taking Rev. Akegarasu's place, try to speak to ourselves. But that is just parroting the teacher. We are attempting to tell others as well as ourselves, "Rev. Akegarasu said such and such ..."

This is like trying to speak for Jesus. Jesus used the word "love," but who else could give the word the same meaning? A western proverb says, "There was only one Christian in the world. He died on the cross."

The only thing Rev. Akegarasu taught us, and taught us with the totality of his being, was

> You should be yourself.

Let us clearly recognize these selves of ours, which are absolutely severed from him.

We should not be so careless as somehow to become Rev. Akegarasu. The teacher does not allow us to imitate him. He is absolutely alone.

Then what should we do? Let us carefully listen to the voice coming from the depth of our being. Let us follow our deepest desires.

The teacher will be watching our activities in this journal with a smile, encouraging us:

> Do whatever you like as fully as possible!

8

Reminiscences

1.   The Propagation of Buddhism

In January, 1946, when I was about to leave Rev. Akegarasu's temple for Nagano,[1] Rev. Akegarasu said,

> Mr. Maida, the propagation of Buddhism is something like throwing two or three drops of coloring material into the muddy stream of the Yangtze River.

2.   An Arrogant Head

Once I guided Rev. Akegarasu into a national sanatorium in Nagano, because I wanted him to talk to the patients there. In the lecture hall the stage was elevated. I had to guide the teacher [who was blind]. At the corner of the stage there was a winding stairway with five or six steps. Furthermore, a slanting wall hung over the stairway like an impending rock. I first climbed the stairs, pulling the teacher's hand very carefully so that he might not lose his step.

After the teacher's talk, coming down from the stage was more dangerous. The winding steps were triangular. It was more difficult to guide a blind man downward. Thus, I focused my full attention on the teacher's every step.

Hardly had the teacher taken one or two steps downward when his forehead hit the impending wall. Then, immediately, he said, "Thank you!" After leading him to a chair, I, feeling guilty, asked him, "Teacher, why did you say 'Thank you' to me?"

His answer was, "Nobody is so kind as you, Mr. Maida, who have taken the trouble to bring my [arrogant] head to the wall and make it bump on it."

3. Appreciation

We invited Rev. Akegarasu to a two-day seminar at the Zenshō-ji temple in Iida, Nagano. When he and I were in the waiting room, the voice of the minister's young wife reached our ears as she played the piano and sang. Then we had the following conversation:

> "Teacher, that is the voice of the minister's young wife. She has such charming eyes. Too bad you cannot see them."

> "But Mr. Maida, do you ever experience a young lady leading you by the hand?"

This was the teacher's spontaneous response.

4. Receiving

Some time before I came to Nagano, I made my first personal visit to Rev. Akegarasu at his temple with Prof. Gyōshō Shimizu, the president of Ishikawa Teachers' College.[2] I accompanied Prof. Shimizu because I was the head professor of the college. In the evening we were led to a tearoom where Rev. Akegarasu treated us to all kinds of delicious food. A good sake called Kinhai was also prepared there. Since it was my first visit there, I hesitated to accept such a feast. When Rev. Akegarasu urged me to eat, I said, "No, thank you." Then the teacher said,

> Mr. Maida, the person who cannot gladly receive a gift from others is a person who cannot gladly give a gift to others.

Thereupon, I immediately changed my mind and devoured all the food offered to me on the table.

5.   Nonsmoking

Immediately after the end of the war, when there was still a shortage of cigarettes, I visited Rev. Akegarasu at his study. The teacher asked me, "Mr. Maida, do you smoke?"

I answered, "Yes, I do."

Then he took out from his drawer a box of cigarettes called Lucky Strikes and gave it to me, saying "Somebody gave this to me." He asked me, "Would you light one cigarette for me?" When I lit a cigarette and gave it to him, the teacher took two or three puffs, slowly savoring its taste. Then, returning the cigarette to me, he said, "Mr. Maida, this is my nonsmoking."

6.   Liberation by the Teacher

From Rev. Akegarasu's writings I selected the articles that touched my heart and published them as a small book entitled the *Lion's Roar*.[3] In one meeting the teacher commented on the publication, saying,

> Mr. Maida is a naughty person. He has made a book that exposes only those things which I wish to hide and not let others know about!

Thereafter, the book's bad reputation was established; it did not sell at all. Rev. Akegarasu's students, who advertised him to the public as "a living Buddha," had to conceal the book, a collection of articles that described only the human—vulgar and animal-like—aspects of the teacher. But I was not disturbed by those articles at all because I believed that each and every word and phrase in them was an authentic expression of the teacher.

Even now I am firmly convinced that there could be no authentic liberation by Rev. Akegarasu other than the liberation by Rev. Akegarasu presented in my book.

7.   Fads

We were in the tearoom of the Myōtatsu-ji temple at Kita-yasuda. Rev. Akegarasu sat in the center of the hearth in the floor. Several of us also sat around it. It was one late autumn evening. In those days the local newspaper was making a big fuss about Jikōson, a man of super abilities, who was visiting Kanazawa City. It reported that a famous sumō wrestler stood on his head when Jikōson ordered him to do so, and so forth. We were laughing and ridiculing the Jikōson fad.

Then, words came out of the teacher's mouth:

> You people are no different! You get my photo and bring it home and put it on a wall. You make this blind man do calligraphy. You are so happy to have it. What you are doing is no different from the Jikōson fad. So what on earth are you saying?

8.   An Offering

Rev. Akegarasu and I were in a train. We had invited the teacher to Nagano and I was taking him from one meeting to another in the prefecture. The teacher said to me,

> Mr. Maida, you are also invited to talk sometimes, aren't you? And at mealtime they serve you food. But if the host gives you the impression that he is offering you a meal reluctantly, that he is giving you a meal that you don't deserve, don't ever touch the meal!

Then he told me about an experience he had in his young days when he lived in the Kōkō-dō dormitory:

> At one time a hotshot speculator was put into prison because of a crime. While in prison, he read my *Lectures on the Tannishō*. After he had served his time, he wrote to me and said that he was deeply moved and saved by the book. He also mentioned that, as a token of gratitude, he wanted to invite me to his house on such-and-such a day. When I went to his house, I found all kinds of delicious food [which had been ordered from a restaurant]. Without touching those dishes at all, I asked him, "Don't you have a wife?"

He answered, "Yes."

So, I told him, "I don't want these dishes. I want to eat whatever your wife prepares." Then, his wife prepared her own cooking after hastily getting some cooked rice from a neighbor's house. I enjoyed it.

9.   An Uninvited Guest

What did Rev. Akegarasu enjoy most in this world? It was giving a Dharma talk. Thus whenever someone invited him for a talk, he never refused the invitation; he somehow managed to put an appointment into his already jam-packed schedule. Besides, if he had an open day, he went uninvited to give a talk. He told his friends, "I am going to your place at such-and-such a time on such-and-such a day. So please hold a meeting and wait for me." Since this uninvited visit was different from a formal invitation, there was sometimes a lack of preparedness on the part of the organizer. For example, it happened that no one was in charge of getting the teacher a meal. In that case, the teacher, though he was hungry, kept on waiting for a meal from morning to afternoon without eating anything. He never asked Miss Nomoto, his secretary who accompanied him, to buy something for him to eat.

Since the teacher never failed to pay his respects to the Rev. Manshi Kiyozawa's tomb at the Saihō-ji temple in Ōhama annually, he talked in Ōhama at least once a year. Ōhama is known as the center of traditionalist Shin followers called Mikawa Dōgyō. They did not appreciate the teacher's talks at all. Thus his visiting there meant going into the midst of total indifference. He was a true "uninvited guest" there. Here I cannot help thinking of the great compassion working in the depths of the teacher's heart. I, a timid person, would not dare to do something like that even once in my life.

It was also when we were on a train in Nagano that he said,

> Mr. Maida, when you go out to talk here and there, you will receive gratuities. But you must also go to a place where they don't give you a penny of gratuity.

10. Without Discrimination

Rev. Akegarasu did many things that I did not understand. The following is one of them.

Rev. Akegarasu once became the executive head of the Higashi Honganji because he could not resist the ardent request. He took the job on the condition that he serve only one year.

When I was first informed that he had accepted the job, I did not understand why he had to take what seemed a job for a politician. But by watching his energetic, extensive activities after taking the position, I realized that my skepticism was unfounded. I also recognized that works of great compassion are carried out in any place without discrimination, be it on a battlefield, in a prison, or in the midst of Hell.

I have earlier mentioned his talks at Ōhama, where he met with total indifference. The teacher used to accept gladly invitations from the learning centers of some of the new religions. Thus it would have been strange if he had refused this invitation from the Higashi Honganji [with which his temple was affiliated]. My small mind could not understand that.

11. "My Water Supply Has Run Out!"

Once I took Rev. Akegarasu to Shigarami, a village on a mountain near Nagano City. We wanted him to give a talk at a family's memorial service. On arriving at the house, he, to his surprise, was informed that they were going to butcher several rabbits to prepare a feast for the ancestors' memorial service where all the relatives and neighbors had gathered. This news was extremely shocking to the teacher, who had previously declared that he would never eat a four-legged animal.

In the evening the teacher started his Dharma talk in a room where all the people had assembled. Miss Nomoto, his secretary, and I excused ourselves from this session and were resting in the next room. It was not until he had spoken ten minutes that I heard the teacher's voice from the next room. He said, "Mr. Maida, my water supply has run out [i.e., words have stopped coming out of my mouth]! Would you finish up my talk?"

Thereupon I hastily changed my clothes to formal wear and went to the room to take the teacher's place. I talked incoherently for about thirty minutes. Then the teacher, who had been listening at my side, said, "Now let me talk" and cheerfully continued his talk.

12. A Record Concert

One day during a seminar at the Myōtatsu-ji temple, the following incident took place.

The Myōtatsu-ji temple had an old electric record player. It also had a worn-out record of Beethoven's Fifth Symphony. During one afternoon session all the seminar attendants were supposed to listen to the record.

When we started to play the symphony, we could hardly hear the sound. Weak, squeaking sound was coming out of the player. Besides, the temple's main hall, wide and empty, was probably the least appropriate place for a record concert. The people who initially gathered in the room with great enthusiasm started to leave one by one, until finally there were only two people in the room. One was the person who was in charge of the player. The other person was Rev. Akegarasu, who was, all by himself, listening very attentively to the half-broken record player.

I was looking at the scene from outside the room. I was telling myself, "What a disaster! We should have checked the player and record in advance!"

The teacher, however, was trying hard to listen to the heart of Beethoven, which existed behind the imperfect and weak sound of the record. He kept on listening to it until the symphony ended. His daily attitude of trying to understand the subtlest movements at the bottom of the human heart was fully manifested in the way he was listening to the record. Thanks to this attitude of the teacher, I was able to have my heart heard by him. Comparing him with the others who had left the room, I could not help thinking "Oh, it is precisely here that a Tathāgata exists!"

I was truly made to recognize the carelessness in my attitude of blaming the imperfection of the player and record rather than the imperfection of my own listening. The teacher was sitting all alone in the main hall of the temple that mid-summer afternoon. I was watching him from afar, roaming around all by myself. There was this kind of secret spiritual communication between the teacher and me.

(1/10, 1967)

13.   The Utmost Limit of Life

I truly revere the fact that Rev. Akegarasu lived at the utmost limit of life. He was continuously travelling, day after day, to give talks. Miss Nomoto, who accompanied him, wanted him to have some rest to save energy for the next day's lectures. When he knew what was in her mind, he said, "Miss Nomoto, are you thinking about such a thing?"

This is how the teacher lived. He tried to use up totally today's power today. He never prepared himself for tomorrow by saving energy for it. He worked hard until late today. If he woke up the next day, he got up. If he did not wake up, he did not get up. He left tomorrow to tomorrow.

One morning, the teacher arrived, by a night train, at Takaoka City in Toyama Prefecture. The main hall of the Shōan-ji temple was packed with many Buddhist men and women. Without taking a moment's rest, the teacher stood on a platform to give a talk. Or, more accurately, he sat on a chair on the platform. Words started to come out of his mouth. But, the pauses between his words became longer and longer until finally words stopped coming out of his mouth. The teacher started to sleep in the chair. Having spoken at various places in Tokyo until the night before, he had come to Takaoka that morning without taking enough rest.

Miss Nomoto, who accompanied him, watched the sleeping teacher for a while. But, realizing that he would not wake up, she told him, "Teacher, why don't you rest in your room this morning and start your lecture this afternoon?"

Answering "Oh, yeah!" the teacher obediently followed her and retired to the waiting room. After taking a hot bath, he had a good sleep during the morning. After lunch, with a cheerful voice, he started to talk to the people who had been waiting for him.

Not long after that, one person who was in the audience told me his impression of the incident. He said, "I saw a living Buddha in the teacher. I could not help putting my palms together to worship him."

In my interpretation, a living Buddha is a person who is living at the utmost limit of life.

There is another similar story. The teacher made it a rule to hold an annual one-week seminar in midsummer. It started August 15. I always went to his temple by the evening of the 14th. He sometimes scheduled a talk in the morning, the afternoon, or even the evening of the 14th; he kept on speaking and working until the last moment. He never saved his energy for the next day, the first day of the one-week seminar, the most important event for him in the year. Without recuperating from his fatigue, he jumped into the morning of the 15th. In this case, too, I saw a teacher who was living at the utmost limit of life.

Several years ago, a person who had insomnia often visited me. He was a schoolteacher. He told me, "If I don't sleep well tonight, it will be bad for tomorrow. So I try very hard to sleep. But the harder I try to sleep, the more difficult it becomes to sleep." Anxiety about the next day's work seems to be a common cause of insomnia.

The sleepless person's life is not built on the idea that the most important thing for him is to use up all his energy doing today's work. His life is shaky, not having a firm basis. He cannot tell himself, "I'll use up all my energy today, and, when exhausted, go to bed! I'll do the same tomorrow. I'll live at the utmost limit of my life, using up all my power!"

If a person is saving his energy for tomorrow, his life seems quite lukewarm to me. Such a person thinks that he will be alive tomorrow.

(9/3, 1966)

14.   The Flexible Mind

From August 15 to 21, I, together with thirty friends of mine from Nagano, participated in the annual retreat held in Rev. Akegarasu's temple in Ishikawa Prefecture. The teacher lectured on Shinran's *Yuishinshō-mon'i* (Essentials of the *Genuine Trust Alone*).

At that time I was again deeply moved by the way the teacher spoke on the platform. He stands on the platform totally empty-handed, without having any preconceived notions. There, on the platform, he, with the totality of his being, is learning from Shinran. Thus each and every word comes out of the learning process; we, the audience, are listening to it. Thus without thinking in advance about what he is going to teach the audience, he utters quite naturally whatever gushes up into his mind in the eternal now of the platform. We, therefore, cannot help seeing him as the embodiment of the flow of eternal life itself, which has no room for fixedness.

What Rev. Akegarasu does on the platform is easier said than done. The teacher is personally practicing the admonishment of his teacher, Rev. Kiyozawa, who told him, "Throughout your life, never *preach* even if you die!" If one speaks about ideas prepared in advance, his talk becomes "preaching" because of its fixedness. But if one talks and learns simultaneously, his talk is genuinely filled with life because of its fluidity.

To stand empty-handed before the Tathāgata—this is not an easy thing. To face everything that happens to us without any preconceived notions—this cannot be done if we do not possess a flexible mind. A flexible mind is selflessness.

Thus it was the Tathāgata that I saw in Rev. Akegarasu when he was speaking on the platform. How noble he was!

(8/31, 1950)

15. "Speak Your Taste of It!"

During one summer retreat, Rev. Akegarasu asked me to give a one-week lecture series under the title "Miscellaneous Impressions of the *Shōbō-genzō*." In the first lecture, I took up one section of the text of the *Shōbō-genzō*. Then, considering that the audience, who had never been exposed to the text, could not understand it, I began explaining its meaning. After listening to me awhile, Rev. Akegarasu said to me, "I don't want to listen to your explanation of the *Shōbō-genzō*! Speak your taste of it!"

"Explanation" means trusting the listener's reasoning power and speaking to convince it. But the teacher did not trust the audience's reasoning power. Much less did he trust his own reasoning. His stance was that he could not find in himself any ability to appeal to the listener's reasoning. Thus in dialog both he and his counterpart exchanged words in a sphere where there was no reasoning. The teacher's talks were precisely like that. Therefore he was not verbose; his words were simple and crisp.

My job, on the other hand, was teaching the students at a teachers' college, who in turn must teach children. Thus Rev. Akegarasu used to tell me, "You are a teacher at a teachers' college! So you are too verbose." By the expression "speak your taste of it!" he meant that I should speak in a sphere where there was no reasoning—where reasoning is not trusted.

In rephrasing the teacher's expression, I would say, "Speak your feeling!" Feeling is not a product of thinking. It is immediate perception, or intuition. It is precisely something experienced by a person who trusts no reasoning power. Thus, imitating the teacher, I often tell a ponderer, "What has come out of your reasoning is a product of your reliance on your own abilities. I don't want to listen to any such thing! Tell me your feeling!"

Genza of Inaba Province[4] started to answer when his questioner had hardly finished his question. Then the questioner said, "Please give me your answer after carefully thinking about it." To this Genza responded,

> The Tathāgata is speaking through my mouth. Together with you,
> I am listening to his words.

These words of Genza show a person whose reliance on his own abilities has totally dropped off.

Thus if, when asked a question, one gives his answer not immediately but after pondering, his answer is not worth trusting because it comes out of his reliance on his own abilities. Since he has figured out the answer with his small brain, it must be full of mistakes.

(8/21, 1953)

9

The Day Japan Lost the War

On August 14, 1945, I was at the Myōtatsu-ji temple in Ishikawa Prefecture to attend [Rev. Akegarasu's] Kita-yasuda retreat, which was to begin on the following day. Late that night Mr. Toyoji Sanada came to the temple from Tokyo. He told Mrs. Akegarasu, "Since I have something very important to tell Rev. Akegarasu, I want to see him immediately." Mrs. Akegarasu reported this to Rev. Akegarasu, who had already fallen asleep in his study. Then the three of us, Mrs. Akegarasu, Mr. Sanada, and I (because Rev. Akegarasu wanted me to come, too) entered his room, which was protected by a large mosquito net. The teacher was sitting upright on a *futon* mat. Mr. Sanada spoke in a small, stammering voice:

> Last night, Mr. Fujimori, a navy captain in Tokyo, told me that it has finally been decided that Japan will surrender unconditionally to the U.S.A. Our emperor himself will announce it over the radio at noon tomorrow. Since I thought Rev. Akegarasu should be the first to know, I have come here in a great hurry. This morning, I was able to buy a ticket to Karuizawa at Ueno station in Tokyo. From Karuizawa I have changed trains one after another and finally have arrived here.

Rev. Akegarasu just said, "Is that so ... ?" He kept silent. (I detected from the teacher's reaction that he did not doubt, even slightly, the truthfulness of Mr. Sanada's report. If I had been in the teacher's position, I might at first have doubted the accuracy of the news.) After a little while, Rev. Akegarasu said, "I am sorry for our emperor. Whatever may happen to us, that's all right, but I hope he stays safe and sound ..." Then he turned to me and said in a resolute tone of voice:

> Mr. Maida, I'll change the topic of the lecture series that begins tomorrow. I'll talk about the *Seventeen-Article Constitution*[1] during this coming week. The only thing that can help us reconstruct Japan is that text. Nothing else can do that.

The moment Rev. Akegarasu listened to the report of the defeat, both the determination to reconstruct Japan and the way to accomplish it came to him just like a flash. What quickness!

The teacher told us, "Please don't tell anybody about this until we have heard the emperor's talk on the radio tomorrow." Then we left his room.

The next day was August 15, the first day of the retreat. At seven in the morning, both those who had come to the temple the day before and those who had got to the temple that morning gathered together in the main hall of the temple. They waited for the appearance of the teacher. None of them knew that that day was a historic day.

After a while Rev. Akegarasu stood on a platform. He looked somewhat sad. He first told his audience that he would talk about the *Seventeen-Article Constitution*, a topic different from the scheduled one. Then, before starting his discussion of the first article of the constitution, he spoke about an incident that had taken place the same morning:

> Mr. N., an old friend of mine, has been living in this temple for several months to recuperate from consumption. Early this morning he killed himself on a railway track near here. As the war situation worsened, Mr. and Mrs. N., who did not have any close relatives, had come to live in this temple, depending on me as his old friend. He probably committed suicide because of depression

over his sickness. My wife was informed of his suicide by the
police. She went out to receive his body and has just returned
home, having taken care of everything ...

The death of a close friend and yesterday's report! The voice of the
teacher, usually so lively and cheerful, was feeble and inaudible. His
one-hour lecture seemed dark, entirely dark.

After the lecture, I had breakfast, left the temple, and rushed to my
parents' house in Kanazawa City. On my way I looked at the summer
sky, clear yet strangely dull, over Kanazawa. Feeling the languid
atmosphere, I whispered, "Is this truly the day Japan has lost the war?"
But as I walked, I had a relieved feeling, as if a heavy load had been
taken off my shoulders.

I told my parents about the previous day's news. I told them to listen
to the radio at noon. Then I went to Ishikawa Teachers' College, my
workplace, which was located at the center of the city. With my
colleagues, I listened to the radio at noon. The emperor's broadcast
announcement was quite unintelligible to everybody. Since I had
some prior knowledge, I could somehow connect the links of his
words and get the general message.

On August 16, the second day of the retreat, Rev. Akegarasu was
totally different from the day before! How cheerfully and powerfully
he talked that morning! He told us:

> I spent all day yesterday in the darkest mood. I was shedding
> tears, mourning our defeat. But this morning, when I was in bed
> about to get up, I heard a voice saying the *nembutsu* [Amida's
> Name]. It came to me like a whisper from nowhere. As soon as I
> heard it, I stood up.

The teacher's voice had a high-spirited tone. Oh, how this tone of
voice continued to resound throughout the last ten years of his life!
How selflessly and dynamically he taught us during those ten years!

During the lunch break that day, the teacher said to me when I went
to talk to him,

> Mr. Maida, up to now, our military officers and political leaders
> have been working very hard on the front line. Now we must ask
> them to withdraw and have a good rest for a while. Instead, we

ministers and educators (I was then head professor at a college) should take their place on the front line. Let's work hard, risking our lives!

These warm yet powerful words resounded like a scolding to me. Even now they are resounding in my ears.

For Rev. Akegarasu, the way to reconstruct Japan was clear from the beginning. It was nothing but regarding Prince Shōtoku's *Seventeen-Article Constitution* as the foundation of the new Japan, and interpreting Shinran's teachings as Shinran's development of Shōtoku's ideas. In the process he hoped to clarify the significance of having Rev. Kiyozawa as his teacher.

Throughout his final ten years, he constantly taught us with a powerful lion's roar. When we see the teacher as a person who wished to reconstruct Japan as Prince Shōtoku's country and transmit Shinran's teachings to the entire world, then, only then, are we seeing the true essence of the living, dynamically working teacher.

(7/14, 1955)

10

August 27

On month x, day x, 19xx, I was separated from Miss K. [who was
Maida's girlfriend in his early twenties]. On August 27, 1954, I was
separated from the Rev. Haya Akegarasu.

On both days I did not shed even one tear. Such cold separations!
Or does separation from a deeply adored one freeze our tears?

I coldly watched Miss K.'s mother. Similarly, I coldly watched the
people who were mourning the death of Rev. Akegarasu. They gave
me a rather repulsive feeling. At the root of my being, currents of dark
blood, of rebellion, were about to surge up. Powerful, irrepressible
impulses were urging me to take action, not allowing me to dwell on
my sorrow. I was about to go forward by stepping on Rev. Akegarasu's
dead body. Like a soldier at the front who, having received a go-ahead
order, goes on by stepping on his friend's dead body, without paying
any attention to it.

I felt sad about being like that. Earlier, when I was determined to
embrace Miss K.'s soul forever, deep in my heart, my external appearance was like ice. Similarly, at the time of Rev. Akegarasu's passing,
when I was determined to keep my teacher's limitless love deep in my

heart and go on all by myself, I was about to kill all ordinary human sentiments and tears and sever all human ties in the secular world. By freezing all my emotions towards other people, I severed my ties with the people surrounding Rev. Akegarasu. By doing this, I hoped to see my teacher face to face and experience complete oneness with him at the innermost place in my heart.

Immediately after Rev. Akegarasu passed away, there was an interesting conversation between Miss N., Rev. Akegarasu's secretary, and Mr. F., a student of Rev. Akegarasu's, concerning the first issue of the journal *Kōsō*.[1] I happened to be there.

> Mr. F.: I would like Mr. Maida to become the managing editor of this journal. He should be the spiritual center of the journal ...
>
> Miss N.: Of course, I agree with you. That's the only possible way.
>
> Mr. F.: Since you were always with Rev. Akegarasu, you must know—did Rev. Akegarasu ever say anything to the effect that Mr. Maida should be his spiritual successor? I assume he did.
>
> Miss N.: As far as I know, Rev. Akegarasu only asked me and his wife to consult with Mr. Maida about the publication of his books. He had absolute faith in Maida in matters concerning publication. But as for the successorship, I at least never heard him say anything.
>
> Mr. F.: Is that so? He didn't express his wishes at all?
>
> Miss N.: (No answer.)

Thus Mr. F. failed to obtain Rev. Akegarasu's "will" to make me the spiritual center of the journal.

After editing the first three issues of *Kōsō* in memory of my teacher, I forced Miss N. to be the managing editor, although she refused. Mr. F. magnanimously made this transition possible.

When Rev. Akegarasu was sick, many people asked who his successor would be. Some people asked me that question. One misguided person went so far as to ask me, "Mr. Maida, you will be his successor, won't you?"

Then I told him, "Why don't you become his successor yourself?"

"A person like myself can't be!"

"Is Rev. Akegarasu not your teacher, then?"

"Yes, he is."

"If you are seeing your teacher face to face, you can't possibly talk about successorship as if it were some other person's problem."

"But for a person like myself, it is so important to learn from the person who succeeds Rev. Akegarasu!"

"Rev. Akegarasu was the one and only person. You are speaking only out of political interest, or for fun. A question about some other person's successorship can't arise for a serious seeker. That's leisurely, idle talk."

"I am seriously asking you this question."

"No. For a person who is seeing the teacher face to face, there cannot be any room for such a question!"

Let me write down the last words I heard from Rev. Akegarasu in this world.

Concerning the publication of his final book, *Transcend This World Together with This World!*, Rev. Akegarasu said,

> This book is the last one I am going to leave this world. So, negotiate carefully with the publisher. Don't be soft on them! Get as much royalty as possible!

I heard these words about one month before his passing, when I visited him at the hospital on my way home from Kyūshū. I knew from these words that he expected to die.

Let me write down *the one and only thing* that I learned from Rev. Akegarasu.

In one discussion session at Rev. Akegarasu's retreat, I, as chairman, asked everyone there, "What one word would you leave this world if you were going to die now? What would be your epitaph for your grave? Would each one of you give us your one word?"

All of a sudden, Rev. Akegarasu, who was sitting beside me, said, "I have one! May I say it?"

"No, teacher, please don't say it until everyone else has said his or her word. If you say it first, it won't be interesting."

"O. K., then, I'll wait."

At the very moment when Rev. Akegarasu said, "I have one!," I knew what he wanted to say.

That one word[2] was *the only teaching* I received from my teacher.

(6/13, 1955)

PART TWO

The Teacher-Student Relationship

11

Reflections on the Teacher-Student Relationship

1. The Greatest Happiness

After we are born in this world, our greatest desire is to meet with a real human being. If we meet one such human being, that's enough. No, it should be only one human being. Our life's purpose is fulfilled by meeting him. The greatest happiness of our lives is found in that meeting.

How, then, can a person meet with such a human being? Unless a person has a sincere desire to see such a human being, he cannot possibly see him. This means that the person must be nurtured to the point where he has a strong desire to see such a person. To be nurtured to that point means that one's life must be genuinely concentrated on seeking a true human being. When sought in such a manner, a true human being will certainly appear. That is true even though each person's karmic conditions for such a meeting are different. It is by this meeting that one's happiness in this world can be consummated.

How sad it is that some people have not yet met with a real human being, have not yet known the truth, and, therefore, have not yet experienced true happiness in their lives! How sad it is that some people end their lives without ever meeting with such a person!

(7/21, 1962)

2. "Learn under a Teacher!"

Creativity within a culture is possible only for a learner. And it is necessarily through *one* person that we can touch our own historical culture. That is why the principle "Learn under a teacher!" is so important. For example, it was Herder [1744–1803, a German philosopher] who shaped and finished the young Goethe.

The person who truly thinks about the essence of a culture learns under a teacher. Those who do not know this will never be able to create a culture.

"Learn under a teacher" expresses the basis of a human being's life as a human being, as a cultural being. It is on this basis that people can find true happiness.

(7/19, 1959)

3. The Dharma Flows between Persons

Mahā-Kāśyapa said to the Buddha, "If I had not met you, the Tathāgata, I would have been a *pratyeka-buddha* and lived in an isolated forest. By fortunately meeting you, I have been able to receive the Dharma communion."[1]

The term *pratyeka-buddha* means a person who is complacent in his dogmatic "awakening." Mahā-Kāśyapa says that if he had not met the Buddha, he would have been trapped in his self-made, dogmatic "awakening."

"By fortunately meeting you, I have been able to receive the Dharma communion" means that Mahā-Kāśyapa, by meeting the Buddha, came to understand the universally valid truth that flows between two persons.

Dharma communion occurs when two people become one in the truth that we are all [foolish] ordinary persons.[2]

90

Mahā-Kāśyapa's realization was possible only after he met his teacher, Śākyamuni. It was possible only in the relationship between a teacher and a student.

I think of Socrates' dialogs. The truth *flows* between two people. "Dharma communion" refers to this.

(1/20, 1960)

4. Spiritual Communion

When does a person generate a desire to become a Buddha? To this question Dōgen answers, "He does so when he experiences spiritual communion with a teacher."[3] Let me discuss spiritual communion in some detail.

First, spiritual communion is an occurrence in the karmic relationship between two human beings. It cannot take place outside a human relationship.

But where can a human relationship be formed that can generate the desire to become a Buddha? It is formed only in a historical situation, within a cultural tradition in history.

A cultural tradition is the tradition of human self-awakening. The tradition of human self-awakening is the self-awakening that was transmitted from one person to another through the ages. Thus spiritual communion means meeting with a real human being. If a person does not meet with a real human being, he cannot generate a desire to become a Buddha. A real human being means a teacher.

Thus if one has not met a teacher, he cannot understand what the desire to become a Buddha is all about. He cannot understand what self-awakening is all about. True self-awakening means experiencing the destruction of the self by meeting a real human being. We can call rebirth from this self-destruction the self-determination of absolute nothingness.

This is how self-awakening takes place. Without meeting a teacher, self-awakening cannot take place. Without such a meeting, the desire to become a Buddha cannot be generated. Hence it is now clear that generating the desire to become a Buddha means true self-awakening, nothing else.

(9/23, 1965)

5. Subjective Nothingness[4]

It is totally useless to read books, sūtras, commentaries, or sayings and judge them by one's arbitrary tastes. Unless all of our human positions are completely smashed to pieces by one person, by a spiritual guide, we cannot possibly understand the subjective nothingness of Śākyamuni. Some people may say that we can understand nothingness only through our intellectual understanding. But unfortunately, that is not real, subjective nothingness. It is absolutely impossible to touch subjective nothingness without meeting with a spiritual guide.

Shinran studied under Hōnen for three years. How harshly, how devilishly, Hōnen must have crushed Shinran during this period, day after day, moment after moment! Thinking about this, I cannot help trembling. But without that, Shinran the independent person would not have been born. It was because Shinran's personality was completely crushed by Hōnen that Shinran respected him as the teacher in his life ... Thus we see that the true appreciation of nothingness is simply the receiving of a teaching. It is shown in the statement, "I, Shinran, do not have even a single disciple" (*Tannishō*, Chapter 6).[5] This is Shinran's nothingness.

(7/6, 1966)

6. Actual Experience

When Dōgen talks about the need to follow a teacher, he naturally has in mind his meeting with his teacher Ju-ching. On meeting his teacher, Dōgen said, "The most important thing in my life, my search for the way, had ended."[6] How could we discuss his awakening experience without talking about this?

Truly meeting with a teacher means only one thing: that one's personality is entirely smashed to pieces before that person. Could there be any authentic religious experience apart from the experience of having one's personality totally blown away? Religious experiences conceived in the heads of scholars have no meaning whatsoever.

Becoming nothingness is not something to be imagined in our mind; it is something which we must actually experience by having our entire self blown away by a teacher. This is true nothingness. Where could we experience true awakening except in meeting a teacher and experiencing this nothingness?

For one thing, true awakening means awakening to the fact that we are the most evil persons in the world. It is not until we awaken to this that we experience nothingness. If some say that they can experience nothingness in Zen samādhi, which is devoid of thoughts or ideas, they could not be more wrong.

(9/29, 1963)

7. Truth Negates

Truth is something we hate. It is uncomfortable and unbearable for us. It contradicts our expectations. It is the negator and assassin of the self. In short, it appears before us as our enemy. What appears agreeable to us is but false. Rev. Kanzō Uchimura [1861–1930, a Japanese Christian thinker] once declared, "All who admire me are my enemies."

Truth appears only as a negator, as an enemy. It never appears as an affirmer, as a friend.

Truth is something diabolical. If you do not perceive its diabolical nature, you do not understand truth. If you see only a single aspect of truth and blind yourself to its destructive character, you have a mistaken notion of truth. You are regarding untruth, something shallow and superficial, as truth.

(5/1, 1966)

8. Attaining Awakening Alone, without a Teacher[7]

Buddhism is quite scientific in that it emphasizes the importance of learning from one's traditional culture. For example, it has the theory of the fifty-three preceding Buddhas.[8]

Śākyamuni found himself in the midst of the history of ancient Indian culture. If the Vedas and the Upaniṣads had not preceded Śākyamuni and had not nurtured him, he would not have existed.

Śākyamuni is known to have attained awakening alone, without a teacher. This, however, does not mean that he was not influenced by his preceding culture. Śākyamuni's attaining awakening alone, without a teacher means that he took a new step forward, after having thoroughly learned from the preceding culture. His new, creative, and unique step forward is called attaining awakening alone, without a teacher.

Likewise, Prince Shōtoku took a new step forward, having learned from Śākyamuni. Shinran took a new step forward, having learned from Hōnen. The same thing can be said about individuals like Beethoven and Goethe. These great individuals could not have existed if they had not learned from their predecessors.

(3/27, 1960)

12

Four Conditions for the Hundred-Eighty Degree Turn in Life

1

The recognition of impermanence liberates all. Liberation means becoming impermanence and working as impermanence itself. In that sense, all existing things are already liberated, just as they are, because they are already working as impermanence itself. Such things as plants, trees, fishes, and insects are already liberated. Only human beings experience (or awaken to) this liberation by recognizing impermanence. For an impermanent being to become aware of being an impermanent being is called recognition.

Thus the crucial question in life can be solved through recognition, not through actions or practice but simply through recognition. That is why it is said that liberation is not a matter of practice (*gyō*), but a matter of understanding (*shin*). It is not in the future; it is in the present moment. Action, or what should be done, has something to do with the future. But liberation is in the eternal now. That is why I say that it is a matter of recognition. It is recognition, nothing else, that immediately enables us to cognize eternal life and thereby know that we are living in the eternal now.

When we go through the hundred-eighty degree turn in life because of recognition, a perfectly free life becomes possible. A perfectly free life is not a practice realized through our efforts; it is something that becomes possible because of recognition.

2

How, then, can we recognize impermanence? It is when the self drops off that recognition takes place. For example, Śākyamuni experienced recognition under the Bodhi Tree [when he attained enlightenment]. Shinran also experienced it when he met his teacher Hōnen. Shinran said, "Having abandoned miscellaneous religious practices, I have taken refuge in the Innermost Aspiration [of Amida]."[1] It was also realized by Dōgen when he was practicing under the Zen master Ju-ching, and this master harshly scolded the monk sitting beside Dōgen. Dōgen then visited Ju-ching and told him, "My body and mind have dropped off."[2] It is said that the Zen master concluded their conversation by telling Dōgen, "[Your attachment to] 'dropped off' must be dropped off, too."

All these individuals show us the hundred-eighty degree turn. It is the hundred-eighty degree turn mentioned in the sentence, "The hundred-eighty degree turn takes place only once in one's life (*Tannishō*, Chapter 16)."[3] Without experiencing this radical change in one's life, the recognition of impermanence cannot be fulfilled in us. So the next question we have to ask is how we can realize the hundred-eighty degree turn.

3

How does the hundred-eighty degree turn take place? It takes place when a person first witnesses the reality of human suffering, of such things as birth, aging, sickness, and death; when he then seeks a way (or method) of transcending suffering; when he searches for a teacher to show him the way; when he investigates the way by following the teacher's instructions; and when he eventually discovers the way. This final discovery of the way is called attaining awakening alone, without a teacher. It is also called authentic personal attainment in which a person understands the real nature of his being all by himself.

In the *Larger Sukhāvatīvyūha-sūtra*, when the Bodhisattva Dharmākara asks his teacher Buddha Lokeśvararāja to show him the way to become a Buddha, the teacher tells him, "You should know it all by yourself."[4] Thus the teacher encourages Dharmākara to attain awakening alone, without a teacher. One must understand or discover the real nature of one's being all by oneself. By meeting Hōnen and studying under him, Shinran eventually experienced attaining awakening alone, without a teacher. And he described his personal experiences in the six volumes of the *Kyōgyōshinshō*, using his own expressions. Śākyamuni is not the only person who experienced attaining awakening alone, without a teacher.

There are four conditions for the hundred-eighty degree turn: the desire to transcend the reality of suffering, the search for the way, the search for a teacher, and personal attainment. All these four are indispensable. Let me discuss each of them in some detail.

4

The desire to transcend the reality of suffering does not occur in a person's mind if he is immersed in the hustle and bustle of daily life. Some quiet moments must be secured in his life. He must treasure those quiet moments and carefully watch the realities in his life. He must be nurtured in an environment or atmosphere that enables him to do this. If some quiet time is not secured for him, he cannot have the mental composure to reflect upon his life.

The desire to transcend the reality of suffering is deeply connected with a person's upbringing. He must be nurtured by his family, local community, and traditional culture. He must be nurtured within a historical context. Without this, the desire to transcend suffering cannot arise. There must be some kind of nurturing by a power beyond the self. In other words, one must be placed in a favorable environment. It is not necessarily an adverse situation that gives rise to the desire to transcend the reality of suffering. The opposite is often the

case; the desire arises in a favorable situation. For example, look at
Śākyamuni.

5

The search for the way is the "seek" and the "knock" in Jesus' words,
"Seek, and it will be given to you. Knock, and it will be opened for
you."[5] Without seeking and knocking, the hundred-eighty degree turn
could not take place. It is only when one seeks and knocks for the way
that the desire to search for a teacher arises. Look at Śākyamuni. Look
at Dōgen. Look at John the Baptist, who searched for Jesus. Or look
at Hōnen.

Śākyamuni was not able to meet his ultimate teacher in life. But he
visited several teachers and studied under them earnestly and sincerely with total devotion. Dōgen travelled all over the great Sung
country in search of the right teacher but he was unable to find him.
When he was waiting in disappointment for a ship on which to return
to Japan, someone suggested that he visit a monk on Mt. T'ien-t'ung.
Because of this accidental karmic condition, Dōgen climbed up Mt.
T'ien-t'ung [where he met his teacher]. Without this karmic condition,
he could not have met his teacher. Hōnen could not find a teacher
among his contemporaries. But after reading a passage[6] in Shan-tao's
Commentary on the Meditation Sūtra, Hōnen declared that he would
rely exclusively on Shan-tao. Thus for Hōnen learning from a scrip-
ture was the same thing as learning under a teacher.

In these individuals we can see the function of karmic conditions—
sometimes karmic conditions help one to meet a living teacher and
sometimes they do not.

6

Personal attainment, the final condition for the hundred-eighty degree
turn, means loss of reliance on one's own abilities. So far one has been
attempting to clarify and grasp the way through his own efforts and
abilities. But now he realizes that the way has already been given by

a power beyond the self. Now he considers all his efforts futile and meaningless; he deserts and abandons them. He starts to live by following the truth [of impermanence] in front of his eyes. He recognizes the simple fact that he is living by becoming the truth—that he is being made to live by the truth. Having this realization is personal attainment. Personal attainment is an experience in which one is totally permeated by the truth and loses reliance on one's own abilities.

This personal attainment became real for Śākyamuni when he looked at the morning star. It became real for Dōgen when he said, "The most important thing in my life, my search for the way, had ended here [when I met the Zen master Ju-ching]." It became real for Shinran when he said, "Having abandoned miscellaneous religious practices, I have taken refuge in the Innermost Aspiration." All these individuals recognized that the truth and everything else had already existed for them. There was nothing for them to do, make, or discover. Everything had already been prepared for them. Everything had been perfectly arranged. Everything had already been finished. Recognizing this and experiencing the total dropping off of the self—this is called personal attainment. This is the hundred-eighty degree turn.

7

The loss of reliance on one's own abilities is called the hundred-eighty degree turn. As far as I am concerned, my body and mind dropped off when I clearly recognized that the truth had already been clarified by Śākyamuni.[7] Up to that time, I had thought that I had to have my own philosophical system or that I had to construct one. But with this realization I felt that a heavy burden was being taken off my shoulders. I did not have to do anything. Everything had already been prepared by Śākyamuni. The truth was perfectly revealing itself through the person of Śākyamuni. There was nothing to be added. The only thing that I had to do was just to follow Śākyamuni, to follow his words. Following him was following the truth itself. It was a revelation of the truth. I unexpectedly encountered the truth in Śākyamuni.

I am not saying that Buddhists should follow Śākyamuni but that they should follow the truth. I just sought the truth. And to my surprise, I suddenly realized that the truth had already been perfectly discovered by Śākyamuni some twenty-five centuries ago. What need was there for my philosophical investigations? The burden on my shoulders was all blown away. With this realization I was reborn. I became a new being, living an easy and relaxed life.

8

We must follow Śākyamuni and experience attaining awakening alone, without a teacher. We must recognize the truth itself. For me, Śākyamuni is a spiritual guide. For Shinran, too, Śākyamuni was a spiritual guide who led him to the truth itself, to Amida. To forget to see the truth itself and rely only on a spiritual guide is so-called inappropriate reliance on (or idolization of) a spiritual guide. A monk of the Bodai-ji temple was the spiritual guide of Genza of Inaba Province. Genza is known as a "wonderful human being (*myōkōnin*)."[8] Genza, however, did not idolize his teacher. Hōnen was the teacher of Shinran. Hōnen was the seventh of the seven patriarchs, as formulated by Shinran, but Shinran did not idolize Hōnen, either.

When the truth was revealed to me through the person of Śākyamuni, I experienced the dropping off of my being. It was my hundred-eighty degree turn. Even now I cannot forget the delightful feeling I experienced when I had that realization—the feeling that all of my burden was immediately taken away. My stubborn idea that I had to construct a philosophical system for myself suddenly disappeared. What an easy, rich, perfect, and harmonious world was given to me through Śākyamuni! At the same time, I saw the whole world in Śākyamuni!

9

Shinran probably experienced this liberating feeling through the *Larger Sukhāvatīvyūha-sūtra*.[9] He must have felt that his burden was immediately lifted. Dōgen must have experienced it through the Zen master Ju-ching. Both Shinran and Dōgen wished to share their personal experiences with others. This desire led to the writing of the *Kyōgyōshinshō* and the *Shōbō-genzō*. They attempted to transmit the truth to others—the truth revealed through Śākyamuni. I feel the same way. I do not worship Śākyamuni simply because he was a great human being. It is the revelation of the truth through Śākyamuni that is crucially important for me.

Before this revelation of the truth my self lost its importance. And this wonderful experience became an important fact in my personal life. That's all. I am not advocating Śākyamuni-ism, Buddha-ism, or Buddha-teaching-ism. There is only one path before me—a path leading to the truth.

10

The solution to the crucial question in life is not easy. When, at the age of nineteen, Genza of Inaba Province witnessed his father's death, his father told him, "After my death, please take refuge in your Real Parent [Amida]." After that, Genza spent ten years writhing in agony as he sought the way. Even the birth of so-called wonderful human beings [who are known for their easy and smooth life-style] involves such difficulties.

In his *Fukan Zazen-gi* (Universal Recommendation of Zen), Dōgen says that even a genius like Śākyamuni had to experience six years of ascetic practice and meditation.[10] Note here that every one of us must diligently seek the way for a long time if we are to solve the crucial question in life. The solution to this question is so important that we cannot ignore it by saying it is too difficult.

I think of the diligent truth-seeking that Jesus probably undertook before he met John the Baptist, before the public life that lasted one year (or three years at most). Although there is no historical information concerning Jesus' earlier life, he must have diligently sought the way before he was thirty. Thus the solution to the crucial question in life is not easy for anybody.

Shinran talked about the Easy Path.[11] But the Easy Path is the spiritual realm of flat-ordinariness [the awareness that one is all right just as he is] that Shinran eventually reached after difficult searching. Thus the Easy Path is not something lazy people might dream about. Furthermore, the Zen master Nan-ch'uan said, "The flat-ordinary mind is the way."[12] His words, too, were a crystallization of a difficult and agonizing truth-seeking process.

(7/19, 1963)

13

The Words of the Good Person

> The good person said, "Just say the *nembutsu* and be liberated by Amida." As far as I, Shinran, am concerned, I just accept and trust his words. That's all.
>
> <div align="right">(<i>Tannishō</i>, Chapter 2[1])</div>

Shinran uses the words "the good person" for his teacher Hōnen. For Shinran, the good person means the one and only teacher in his life, the teacher from whom he learns with the totality of his being. The relationship with the good person is comparable to the relationship of a woman with her future husband, the man with whom she falls in love and with whom she becomes united. The term "the good person" (*yokihito*) is cognate with the term "the sublime person" (*kajin*). What a good expression "the good person" is! I appreciate the subtle nuances of the Japanese word.

The teacher-student relationship is like falling in love with another human being and abandoning one's entire being to that person. Rev. Kanzō Uchimura devoted his entire life to Christianity because he happened to meet a Christian missionary at the Farming School in Sapporo. With his disposition, Rev. Uchimura, who was exclusively devoted to Jesus, could have been exclusively devoted to Shinran. There is evidence to support my saying so in his article, "The Friends of My Faith—Genshin, Hōnen, and Shinran."[2]

It is only *accident* that determines to whom one entrusts oneself. No woman can say that she had already, at her birth, decided whom she would choose as her husband. Likewise, no one can tell beforehand whom he will trust as his teacher. Thus accident plays a crucial role in deciding to trust someone. If there are no accidents involved, there is no real feeling of trust.

It is precisely because of accidents that we have the trembling experience of throwing away the entirety of our being—that we experience a feeling of leaping into the abyss. Thinking that the die has been cast, one can easily entrust one's entire life to the teacher and engage in dynamic truth-seeking in which one's entire body and life are forgotten. Accident is the very thing that gives life to trust.

Our love of someone cannot be controlled. It is not a matter of ethics. It is beyond our intention and design. We could call it the working of the Tathāgata or an inconceivable karmic event. Be that as it may, it is the working of a power which is beyond human power. It is a *breakthrough opening* to the great life of the universe, and we are facing it. This breakthrough opening, or one crucial experience, is an accident.

Although the breakthrough opening is an accident, it leads to the great life of the universe. The life of the universe is real—it is the only reality. Our touching upon it or being supported by it is not an accident; it is, when viewed from the standpoint of universal life, inevitable. Here is the inevitable aspect of genuine trust. Genuine trust has a firm and immovable aspect that nothing can shake or disturb. Indeed, it should be said that genuine trust does not retrogress.[3]

The teacher-student relationship, described as "accepting and trusting the words of the good person," is analogous to the love relationship discussed above. We can understand it from the love relationship. But there is one difference. In the case of the love relationship, the person we love is important. But in the case of the teacher-student relationship, it is the Dharma, which shines through the teacher, that is important. "Accepting his words" is important. Shinran saw Amida Buddha in Hōnen. He was not simply seeing a person named Hōnen.

So-called inappropriate reliance on the teacher occurs when one does not see the Dharma in the teacher. The Dharma is the most important thing in the teacher, not his personality or human qualities. The Dharma—"Just say the *nembutsu* and be liberated by Amida"—is the most important thing. We must immediately go to the Dharma which the teacher embodies. We must see the Dharma, not the person. We must have a direct encounter with the Tathāgata.

Here the Dharma is the great life of the universe. That is what we should pay attention to. That is what we should rely upon. It is not a person. The teacher does not tell us, "Come to me!" He always tells us, "Go to the Dharma through me!" We should not forget this even for a second. The teacher is a breakthrough opening through which the Dharma—the life of the universe—contacts us.

The teacher makes us awaken to the great universal life. In a man's love of a woman, his relationship with this life is, to use Hegel's terminology, *an sich* (in itself). But in the case of the teacher-student relationship, the student's relationship with this great universal life is *für sich* (for itself)—a matter of self-awakening. The teacher does not make the student rely upon the teacher. He makes the student rely upon the great universal life and thereby attain true independence. Independence through relying upon the great universal life—this is the content of genuine trust.

There is a deep reason for the words which Shinran states resolutely at the beginning of the sentence—"As far as I, Shinran, am concerned." The teacher is a person who makes us independent. He is "the good person" in the true sense of the word.

(6/28, 1950)

105

14

"Even If I Were To Be Deceived"

Dōgen uses the expression "Being fallible, one takes refuge in fallibility."[1] This sounds as if one should make one mistake after another! But on the contrary, a commentary on the *Shōbō-genzō* says,

> The words "Being fallible, one takes refuge in fallibility" describe the content of liberation.[2]

I want to interpret these words of Dōgen through the second chapter of the *Tannishō*.

First, the "fallible" in "being fallible" refers to the self. It refers to the "I" (Shinran), which is mentioned in the following italicized phrase:

> *I am totally ignorant* as to whether the *nembutsu* is truly the cause of my attaining birth in the Pure Land or whether it is a karmic action because of which I must fall into Hell.[3]
>
> (*Tannishō*, Chapter 2)

Is this "I" not fallibility itself, or delusion itself?

Next, the "fallibility" in "takes refuge in fallibility" refers to the other. It refers to Hōnen, Shinran's teacher, whom Shinran discusses in the following italicized phrase:

Even if I were to be deceived by Hōnen Shōnin, even if I were to fall into Hell because of saying the *nembutsu*, I would not regret it.[4]

(*Tannishō*, Chapter 2)

Why is Hōnen "fallibility"? Because he may deceive Shinran. It is possible that he may cheat him. Having the potential to cheat people is fallibility itself.

Here Shinran does not understand Hōnen as a person who is without fallibility, nor as a person who is absolutely infallible. Since Shinran's eyes are totally muddled by desires and passions, the image of Hōnen which is reflected in his eyes is unclear and blurred. Since Shinran wears a pair of colored glasses, the Hōnen whom he sees is of the same color. To Shinran's fallible eyes, his teacher also appears as fallible. Thus Shinran's relationship with Hōnen can be described with "Being fallible, one takes refuge in fallibility."

There is only fallibility in their relationship, nothing else. Fallibility is the only reality there. It is total and genuine fallibility. That is why the commentary says, "These words ... describe the content of liberation."

But suppose Shinran had said, "Hōnen is an absolutely infallible person." What would that mean? It would mean that there is a dichotomy there, that fallibility (darkness) and truth (brightness) are being contrasted. In such a relationship there cannot be liberation.

If Shinran were to see Hōnen that way, that would be quite strange. It would mean that Shinran, who identifies himself as fallible, was claiming to have certain and infallible judgement concerning Hōnen, his teacher. Then Shinran's fallibility would not be genuine fallibility. But the reality is that Shinran is going to Hōnen without being able to know whether Hōnen is a true teacher or not.

To use my expression, Shinran is saying, "I may be mistaken, but I am going to Hōnen." This is how it is when one commits one's life to another. Genuine trust is a matter of life, not of judgement. "Being fallible, one takes refuge in fallibility" is life going to life. It is, as it were, an unconditional union of two lives. It is called genuine trust.

For example, think about a woman who is to marry a man. Since she is going to entrust her life to him, it will be an unconditional union of two lives. Thus, it is a concrete manifestation of genuine trust.

Further, we can say the same thing about all human unions. For example, when we ride a bus, we entrust our lives to the bus driver, a complete stranger. Thus we know that a person's union with another person is "a meeting of absolutely unique, separate entities,"[5] a bridging of the absolutely unbridgeable, or a logically inexplicable union. Since every union of two individuals is a bridging of the absolutely unbridgeable, we may call it genuine trust. As the entire world consists of such unions, this world should be called the world of genuine trust. We are already living in the world of genuine trust. Genuine trust is seen everywhere, not only in unions between men and women.

Talking about the teacher-student relationship again, I wish to ask, "Don't we often regard our teacher as a 'true' teacher? But don't we go to him without knowing if he is a true teacher or a false one?" "Being fallible, one takes refuge in fallibility" is the only basis for the true teacher-student relationship. If this single-minded relationship does not exist, there cannot be a *true* teacher.

It is not because we regard a person as a true teacher that a true teacher exists. That a person is a true teacher is spontaneously revealed only when "being fallible, one takes refuge in fallibility," that is, when the student and the teacher are one, and the student cannot tell whether his teacher is true or false.

The words "Being fallible, one takes refuge in fallibility" express ideal single-minded devotion. That is why this expression is said to be "the content of liberation."

Can we define ourselves as something other than fallible? Prince Shōtoku said, "My foolish mind cannot understand it."[6] Shinran called himself "a foolish bald-headed person."[7] They knew themselves to be fallibility itself. In what else besides fallibility could we (who are fallible) take refuge?

We may be mistaken, but we cannot help taking refuge in fallibility. Is this not the basic way we live? Is this not the principle underlying human life? "Being fallible, one takes refuge in fallibility" reveals the basic nature of life. Life is genuine trust. I cannot help commenting that "Being fallible, one takes refuge in fallibility" describes the content of genuine trust. We actually base our lives, moment after moment, on "Being fallible, one takes refuge in fallibility."

By extracting "Being fallible, one takes refuge in fallibility" from the *Shōbō-genzō*, I have attempted to explain that Dōgen and Shinran are basically one and the same. How do people who consider Zen and Shin to be different interpret this expression?

Zen considers enlightenment the most important thing and identifies it with fallibility. How honorable fallibility is! Fallibility, indeed! This one word "fallibility" is the essence of Dōgen. Prince Shōtoku spoke of the same thing when he used the term "a [foolish] ordinary person." Shinran further wrote of "a [foolish] ordinary person who is filled with desire and suffering." Our liberation depends on whether we can identify ourselves with this fallibility or not. Could I be something other than fallible? Could all the people in the world be anything other than fallible? I truly appreciate the comment "'Being fallible, one takes refuge in fallibility' describes the content of liberation."

I have said that "Being fallible, one takes refuge in fallibility" is the principle underlying human life. "Fallible" refers to the self. "Fallibility" refers to the other. Thus "Being fallible, one takes refuge in fallibility" is oneness between self and other. Hence we recognize that this world is a place where all things manifest one truth, the truth of fallibility. With this realization, we discover that we are dwelling in a peaceful and bright world. We discover that we are already liberated. Here fallibility is absolute fallibility.

(10/10, 1955)

15

"I, Shinran, Do Not Have Even a Single Disciple"

Even the statements of our revered predecessors become a matter of objective logic, if we place two or more of the statements before our eyes. If we do so, our main concern is not receiving teachings. We are just interested in discussing our predecessors' words, not in self-examination.

If we are to quote our predecessors, we should quote only one statement. And our individual self should squarely and honestly confront the statement. Our self should be laid on the table for examination and should be carefully scanned by the predecessor's sharp words of wisdom. If that is done, we are truly receiving teachings.

If I say, "Shinran said this, these words of Jesus are similar, and Dōgen expresses the same idea from a different angle like this," then I am like a person who is displaying various things in a showcase. I am simply joining the ranks of spectators. This self of mine alone should receive teachings.

What is the use of investigating and clarifying the logical connection between some statement of one predecessor and some statement of another? What is the use of it when it is my individual liberation that is crucial? The same thing can be said about the historical connections between various statements. The important thing about a predecessor's statement is not its historical connection with another predecessor's statement but whether his statement is actually saving this soul of mine. Such things as logical investigations and historical studies are the useless undertakings of leisurely people who do not need liberation.

Readers of the *Kyōgyōshinshō* can easily fall into the danger of useless investigations. We should rather confront the reality of our selves at this very moment by facing a bloody cross section of our lives, through the *Tannishō*. I am grateful that the *Tannishō* is a collection of fragmentary statements, because this eliminates the danger, into which we may so easily fall, of seeing the text from the standpoint of objective logic.

What is the use of saying, "Shinran called himself 'Foolish Bald-headed Shinran' because Hōnen called himself 'Stupid Hōnen.' Furthermore, we can find the sources of these self-descriptions in Prince Shōtoku's writings. In his commentary on the *Lotus Sutra*, Prince Shōtoku says, 'My foolish mind cannot understand it.' In the tenth article of the *Seventeen-Article Constitution*, he also says, 'We are all [foolish] ordinary persons' "? It is enough if we face one of these self-descriptions and it immediately smashes our delusions to pieces. If I am truly made to know my foolish bald-headedness, can there be any room for knowledge about the lineage, history, and logic of foolish bald-headedness?

Nicolaus Cusanus [1400–64, a German mystic philosopher] talked about "knowledge of ignorance" [*docta ignorantia*].[1] If we see it objectively, it is no longer knowledge of ignorance; it is knowledge of knowledge of ignorance. Knowledge of ignorance is simply bowing our heads and saying, "I am ignorant." Likewise, what use is there in *knowing about* the fact that Shinran called himself Foolish Bald-headed Shinran? And how much less meaning there is in knowing about the tradition, lineage, history, and logic of this statement!

When we quote the classics, the words of our predecessors, the mind that wishes to quote a passage must be carefully examined. In traditional Buddhist debate, the person who first quotes a classic is judged the loser. I think that is quite significant.

Furthermore, even if we quote the classics, do we really understand them? Jesus used the word love. So I can quote the word love. But, there is a million-mile difference between his love and my love. Someone aptly said, "There was only one true Christian. He died on the cross."

I hate those who quote their predecessors' statements one after another. I cannot help wondering if they, by quoting their predecessors' words, are somehow placing themselves on the same level as those predecessors.

As far as our liberation is concerned, I feel that we should always have only one teacher. Thus I am not uncomfortable because the Rev. Kanzō Uchimura frequently quotes the words of Jesus. He regards Jesus as his only teacher and is always confronting him face to face.

Likewise, I am not unhappy at all at seeing Shinran cite many quotations in his *Kyōgyōshinshō*. He does it because he is always seeing the Tathāgata, confronting him, and consulting him. Otherwise, he could not possibly have made his sudden and spontaneous confession at the end of the volume on *Shin*, the one in which he says, "I know this from the bottom of my heart: How sad it is! Foolish Bald-headed Shinran ..."[2] It is impossible to find that kind of spontaneous confession in the middle of scholars' treatises. All those quotations that Shinran cites are the words of the Tathāgata alone.

The one thing that is important is that I alone, nobody else, receive the teachings. I must always confront my teacher [Rev. Akegarasu] face to face. When I forget this basic attitude, I start to preach the Dharma to others. I fall into a teacher-mentality or preacher-mentality.

I cannot help saying to myself "I must keep on learning from my teacher. I am the only person who is left to be liberated in this world." When I say this to myself and clearly recognize my situation, I suddenly discover that I have already been liberated. This is indeed an inconceivable liberation. I have learned this from Shinran's words, "I, Shinran, do not have even a single disciple."

16

The Negation
of One's Teachership

In the *Tannishō* (Chapter 6) Shinran says,

> Some single-minded *nembutsu* practitioners are competing with each other, saying, "This is my disciple and that is his disciple." This is utterly outrageous.
>
> I, Shinran, do not have even a single disciple. For if I, by my own contrivances, could make someone say the *nembutsu*, then he might be my disciple. But it would be preposterous to call a person "my disciple" when he is moved to say the *nembutsu* by Amida.
>
> People meet because karmic conditions cause them to meet. People separate because karmic conditions cause them to separate. Thus people should not say that if one leaves one teacher and says the *nembutsu* under another, he cannot attain birth in the Pure Land. Are they saying that they can take back the genuine trust [or understanding] which was given by the Tathāgata as if it were given by them? Such things should not be said.
>
> If one is in accord with the principle of naturalness, he will surely feel grateful for the magnanimity of the Buddha's compassion and for his teacher's compassion as well.[1]

My interpretation of this chapter is as follows:

> Some single-minded *nembutsu* practitioners are competing with
> each other, saying, "This is my disciple and that is his disciple."
> This is utterly outrageous.

"Some single-minded *nembutsu* practitioners" means those who have
despaired of improving themselves by their own efforts because they
have found those efforts to be ineffectual. As a result, they have
no means of liberation but to recite the *nembutsu*. During this
process they have to learn a teaching. But when they find joy in it,
they wish to transmit it to others. Then discrimination arises—"This
is my disciple and that is his disciple." This discrimination derives
from the desire to control others. As a consequence, groups are
formed, and fights among them start. Since each group wishes to
control other groups, it is natural that "competition" and disputes
arise.

How little connection there is between experiencing liberation
through the way of the *nembutsu* and engaging in a dispute! Yet "most
people form groups and very few reach the true way,"[2] as Prince
Shōtoku stated in the first article of his *Seventeen-Article Constitution*. This is a human reality. This is why genuine religion deteriorates
into the so-called "new religions."

What causes conflict among the people who say, "This is my
disciple and that is his disciple"? It is the difference in their doctrines.
It also gives rise to sects. If different doctrines were not established,
people would not argue.

Doctrine becomes necessary for a person who assumes the position
of a teacher. How far removed such a person is from the fundamental
religious experience—that one experiences liberation through the
way of the *nembutsu*! How far removed he is from the universal
religious experience—that one experiences complete liberation
through religion!

By opposing the advocating of doctrines, Shinran clarifies what
real religious experience is. He also implicitly discusses the issue
of groups and of the power to control others that groups claim to
have.

Shinran sharply denies "doctrines," "groups," and "the power to control others." He says, "It is utterly outrageous." This is total negation.

I, Shinran, do not have even a single disciple.

Shinran says that he is an entirely [foolish] ordinary person who is loaded with deep karmic evil. This [foolish] ordinary person of the lowest type has experienced liberation by meeting with the great compassionate Aspiration [or Vow] of Amida Buddha [to liberate all sentient beings]. This was Shinran's fundamental religious experience. And he, throughout his life, never departed from this vital experiential view of life. He always confronted the reality of his life, the bloody cross section of his life.

Shinran, in the postscript of the *Tannishō*, expresses the same experience by saying, "When I carefully think about the Vow that Amida Buddha made after five kalpas of meditation, I realize that it was made for myself, Shinran, alone. How grateful I am for the Vow designed to liberate me, though I am loaded with deep karmic evil!"[3]

Shinran is the only person to be liberated. How could he assume the position of a teacher, which is secondary? How could his "doctrine" be formed? How could his "group" or "power to control others" arise? In the same postscript, he says, "I am totally ignorant as to what is good or evil."[4] Without knowing what is good or evil, how could he regulate his "group"? How could he establish "doctrines" on which to base a group?

Shinran always confessed before others his personal and subjective experience of liberation. It was of primary importance in his life. He had neither a doctrine nor a group. He always maintained his position as "myself, Shinran, alone."

Although some people regard Shinran's *Kyōgyōshinshō* as a text on his doctrine, his purpose in writing it was so that he, Shinran, alone, could keep on learning from his predecessors. The full title of the *Kyōgyōshinshō* is *Passages Concerning Teaching, Practice, and Attainment, Which Reveal the Truth of the Pure Land, Selected by Shinran, a Disciple of Śākyamuni*.[5] This title indicates that Shinran had selected passages written by his predecessors. It explains how this very unusual book, ninety percent of which consists of quotations, was born. Those who see this book as a text in which Shinran systematized doctrine to be taught to others totally misunderstand the nature of the book.

> For if I, by my own contrivances, could make someone say the
> *nembutsu*, then he might be my disciple.

Shinran says that he cannot, by his own efforts, make someone say the *nembutsu*. He says so because the *nembutsu* is an absolute, or one-to-one, confrontation between Amida Buddha and each human being. Nobody is allowed to come between the two.

Shinran stood before Amida Buddha all by himself and experienced absolute liberation. And he simply confessed this experience in his writings. Whether his confession would make others say the *nembutsu* or not was none of Shinran's concern. Thus he said, "Such is the understanding of the foolish person that I am. Beyond this, whether you take up the *nembutsu* and entrust yourself to it, or reject it, is entirely your own decision."[6] Whether or not others, having listened to Shinran's confession and learned about his personal liberation experience, stand before Amida face to face, depends on their respective individual backgrounds and circumstances. There cannot be any Amida-Shinran-disciple relationship (in which Shinran is an intermediary between Amida and a disciple). Such a relationship would indicate that Shinran forgot his studentship and assumed the position of the Buddha vis-à-vis his disciple. Shinran, who identified himself as the lowest type of person, a person who must keep on learning, would never do this.

Instead of disciples, Shinran had fellow learners and fellow practitioners. He had friends with whom he shared the joy of genuine trust experienced in the *nembutsu*.

The *nembutsu* is absolute; it is the Dharma. Thus Shinran could not use the *nembutsu* as a means to liberate others. If he could use it as a means, it could not be absolute; it could not have the power to liberate him. Since he could not use the *nembutsu*, the *nembutsu* is absolute and has absolute power. Because the *nembutsu* is absolute, he said that he could not have a disciple.

> But it would be preposterous to call a person "my disciple" when
> he is moved to say the *nembutsu* by Amida Buddha.

How, then, does a person come to say the *nembutsu*? He comes to say
the *nembutsu* because Amida uses everything in this world as a means
to move him to do so. Since the *nembutsu* is the absolute Dharma,
absolute power, it becomes the world itself and exerts its power over
him.

Because the *nembutsu* is absolute, because Amida uses all of this
world to move a person to say the *nembutsu*, a person utters the
nembutsu in a direct relationship with Amida, without any
intermediary.

The fact that Shinran made confessions and a person hears them is
certainly one part of the infinite network of causes that eventually
makes a person say the *nembutsu*. But such things are absorbed by and
disappear into the infinite and absolute whole. Being finite, they
become negligibly small before the infinite.

Could one, on the basis of what he has done for others, claim, "I
made him say the *nembutsu* and he is my disciple"? Such a claim is
"preposterous." It reflects conceit, arrogance, impudence, and lack of
self-reflection.

The *nembutsu* is a direct relationship between Amida and a human
being. That is how Shinran experienced it in his personal life. That is
why he wrote the words quoted above: "When I carefully think about
the Vow that Amida made after five kalpas of meditation, I realize that
it was made for myself, Shinran, alone." Here there is only a direct
relationship between Amida and Shinran; nobody else is intervening.
What, then, was Hōnen for Shinran? What were the seven patriarchs
for him? As far as Shinran was concerned, they represented Amida.
He did not see them as human beings. He just relied on Amida, on one
Buddha. He did not idolize his spiritual guides and was not attached
to them.

> People meet because karmic conditions cause them to meet. People
> separate because karmic conditions cause them to separate. Thus
> people should not say that if one leaves one teacher and says the
> *nembutsu* under another, he cannot attain birth in the Pure Land.

This world, as a whole, is a world of karmic conditions. The world, as a whole, is moving by itself. It has its own laws which are unknown to human beings. This world is moving because of causes of its own, for which Spinoza [1632–77, a Dutch philosopher] used the term "self-cause" (*causa sui*). Śākyamuni called these causes "impermanence." We may also call them conditional arising or dependent origination. Karmic conditions are inconceivable because the temporal and spatial elements that form this world are limitless.

"Karmic conditions that cause people to meet" are one phase of the movement of this world. So are "karmic conditions that cause people to separate." Thus, meeting and separation are both caused by inconceivable karmic conditions.

Thus the statement "If one leaves one teacher and says the *nembutsu* under another, he cannot attain birth in the Pure Land" is totally against the laws of this world. All things are in the hands of Amida (the absolute one). Amida is using this entire world as a means to liberate sentient beings; we cannot know what is in Amida's mind. Much less can we possibly assert, "If you do this, you will not attain birth in the Pure Land." Thus Shinran says, "People should not say [this]." He says that people cannot find any grounds for a statement like this.

I have said that this world is a world of karmic conditions. This means that Amida, who is nothing but karmic conditions, is moving human beings. How can a human being, who is only one finite link in the endless chain of karmic conditions, come up with a decisive judgement or conclusion about the way Amida liberates people?

> Are they saying that they can take back the genuine trust [or understanding] which was given by the Tathāgata as if it were given by them? Such things should not be said.

Genuine trust [or understanding] is given to us directly by the Tathāgata [Amida]. It is transferred to us by the Tathāgata. Genuine trust [or understanding] is recognition of the truth. The truth itself calls us. It makes us intuit and recognize it.

The Tathāgata is the truth itself. Because in Buddhism the truth is synonymous with human awakening, the truth can be symbolized by the Tathāgata [one who is awakened to the truth], the absolute other. This Tathāgata can make us recognize the truth.

The truth is beyond our subjectivity, beyond our selves. It is the objective truth—the absolute other—that smashes our subjectivity. It cannot be appropriated by us. As I mentioned earlier, we cannot use it as a means to liberate others. If we could use it, it would not be the absolute truth.

Shinran says, "Are they saying that they can take it [genuine trust] back as if it were given by them?" Here Shinran is asking those people if they can give others recognition of the truth (or genuine trust) and take it back freely as if it were their own possession. Both genuine trust and the *nembutsu* that comes out of genuine trust are not relative matters that can be controlled by our subjective and arbitrary likes or dislikes.

Thus Shinran says, "Such things should not be said." He is challenging such people by saying, "What are you thinking about? What are you misunderstanding?" He is not saying, "You should not do [what you imply you can do]." If he were saying that, it would indicate that they could do it if they wanted to. Here he is telling them to realize that it is impossible to do something like that.

> If one is in accord with the principle of naturalness, he will surely
> feel grateful for the magnanimity of the Buddha's compassion
> and for his teacher's compassion as well.

"If one is in accord with the principle of naturalness" means "If one selflessly follows the principle of naturalness." This indicates that the people whom Shinran criticizes are unnatural. Why are they unnatural? Because those who should be students are behaving as teachers. Because those who should kneel in their joy at being liberated by Amida are attempting to teach others from a higher position.

Thus "being in accord with the principle of naturalness" means becoming a kneeling person. It means revering the absoluteness of liberation by Amida or selflessly following the absolute truth. It means constantly staying in the fundamental religious experience expressed in the statement "I, Shinran, do not have even a single disciple."

Thus one constantly experiences the joy of liberation in the here and now. Our liberation, our encounter with Amida's compassion, is eternally new. It always takes place in the present moment and so is always lively and fresh. It can be experienced only by the naive spirit of a beginner. Thus Zeami [1364–1443, a master of the Noh theater] said, "Don't forget the beginner's mind!"[7] It is the fundamental religious experience.

"The principle of naturalness" is the principle of life. It is the true nature of life. It is life. It is the true nature of reality, or the true principle. After all, it is truth itself.

Thus "to be in accord with (the principle of naturalness)" is recognition (of the truth). In other words, it is that recognition of the absolute other that is making us exist here. This recognition is our liberation. Here we feel reverence for the power that liberates us one-sidedly, without anything being required of us. Thus we "feel grateful for the magnanimity of the Buddha's compassion." We also revere the personal power of the teacher who has guided us to liberation by the Buddha. Hence Shinran says, "one will certainly feel grateful for the magnanimity of the teacher's compassion as well."

"Magnanimity of compassion" implies a selfless feeling—the feeling that one's entire being is unconditionally embraced and absorbed by the liberating power of the Buddha.

"Feeling grateful for the magnanimity of compassion" is the natural way of life. It is the life-style of a person who entrusts himself to the absolute power beyond the self. The truth about our life is that we are made to exist by an absolute power beyond the self. When one experiences liberation, one naturally comes to recognize this truth.

In the last analysis, "feeling grateful for the magnanimity of the Buddha's compassion and for the teacher's compassion as well" is the kneeling mind. This kneeling mind is said to be naturalness. When one becomes a teacher and attempts to teach, there is no truth. It is rather when one becomes a student and reveres a teacher that "the principle of naturalness" exists. In this way, the relationship between teacher and student can be formed. It is always when one completely kneels down that a natural teacher-student relationship can be formed. This relationship is not based on doctrine or on educational need. Much less is it based on the desire to control a group. It is based on one's desire to live a true life.

(10/4, 1956)

17

Worship

Recently I read a book by a certain religious philosopher. His book left an extremely bad aftertaste. It also made me reflect upon myself. Hence I want to write about my impressions of the book.

Some time ago I read Mr. Shigeo Hayashida's book *The Tannishō Smears Shinran.* The aftertaste of this book was also extremely bad. I felt that Mr. Hayashida must have considered himself the only impeccable person who does not smear Shinran. Another reason for the bad aftertaste was that I recalled the Rev. Haya Akegarasu's words about another book of Hayashida's entitled *The Human Shinran.* Concerning this book, Rev. Akegarasu said, "I cannot talk about the human Shinran. If books do not have such titles as *Learning from Shinran Shōnin,* or *Revering Shinran Shōnin,* or *In Praise of Shinran Shōnin,* I do not regard them as worth reading and would not read them."

The book on religious philosophy that I recently read also contains criticism of Shinran. An author who is able to criticize Shinran, I thought, must be a truly great person. But I wondered what was the source of his criticism. I asked myself if I could criticize Shinran.

Then I discovered that I was far from criticizing him. The same thing can be said about Dr. Kitarō Nishida. In his articles, Dr. Nishida talks about Shinran with absolute respect. He does not seem to think it possible to criticize Shinran. He is kneeling before him. It was with this deep respect that he wrote his *Collection of Articles No. 7.*[1]

I have said that this book on religious philosophy criticizes Shinran. I do not think it bad to criticize people. Criticism is all right if the criticizer fully understands the person he is criticizing. Likewise, one may criticize a religious personality only if one fully understands the essence of religion.

What, then, is the essence of religion? To answer this question, let me cite the Five Gates of Mindfulness as formulated by the Bodhisattva Vasubandhu [ca. A.D. 300–400]. They are: (1) worship, (2) praise, (3) vow making, (4) meditation, and (5) merit transferring. Notice that the first of these five gates is worship. If one does not know worship and yet speaks about religion, one is not actually talking about religion at all. The author of the book on religious philosophy is not truly bowing his head before Christianity or Buddhism. There is no worshipping in him.

Talking about religion without worship is like talking about the internal structure of a house without entering the gate of the house. It does not touch religion at all. To touch religion is quite simple. One must simply bow one's head. If one does not enter the gate but discusses religion, one is discussing religion without actually touching it.

In Buddhism there is a story about blind men who touch an elephant. One blind man touches the belly of the elephant and says, "An elephant is like a wall." Another blind man touches its tail and says, "An elephant is like a rope." Other blind men touch its tusk, leg, and nose and say various things. Although their impressions are funny, they are at least touching the elephant. But the author of the book has not even touched the elephant of religion and is nonetheless discussing it. So he is more comical than those blind men.

I cannot help making up another parable.

Once there was a blind man. He came to a spot where an elephant was tied to a pole. To find out what an elephant was like, he touched the pole. He said, "An elephant is like a long piece of wood." Then he started an extensive discussion of the elephant.

18

Self-Awakening

"Studying the Buddha's path is studying the self."
                                  (Dōgen, *Genjō Kōan*)

"The Buddha's path" refers to actions that we take in continuous pursuit of the ideal. It is idealistic action. We may call it "seeking the path."

The Buddha's path is not a fixed path. Since it is the action of continuous seeking, it is dynamic. Thus Kenji Miyazawa [1896–1933, a Japanese poet] explained it with the expression, "Seeking the path is the path."[1]

As far as the path is concerned, predecessors have trodden it. The word "path" does not vaguely refer to the mere existence of a path; it refers to the existence of a path that people have travelled. Apart from people, there is no path. More accurately, the predecessors who have travelled the path are themselves the path. Apart from them, there is no "Buddha's path." Thus the Zen master Dōgen often uses the term, "the life-style of a Buddhist patriarch (*busso no anri*)."

Look at how children grow up. Without imitating their parents or older children, they cannot grow up. The same thing can be said about the history of mankind. The existence of predecessors is indispensable to the social life of mankind.

Thus the Zen master Dōgen uses the word "studying (*narau*)." The word "studying" is synonymous with "learning (*manabu*)," which derives from the word "imitating (*manebu*)." Learning means imitating the life-styles or methods by which predecessors pursued their ideals.

For example, look at art students. They spend time copying pictures. Listen to Bashō [1644–94, a Japanese haiku poet]. He said, "First, enter the standard rules and then exit from them." Entering the standard rules means imitating. It was not until Ryōkan [1758–1831, a Japanese Zen monk] had wholeheartedly studied Chinese handwriting texts that he developed his incomparable art of calligraphy. Further, it is obvious that Goethe learned much from Dante, and from Shakespeare, before he wrote his *Faust*. If someone thinks that he can come up with a new creation without learning from his predecessors, he is a fool. The necessary, indispensable basis for creativity is imitating.

What a humble expression Dōgen's "studying" is! He would not have uttered this word if he had not knelt down before a predecessor, having his self reduced to nothing. Dōgen shed such heartfelt tears of joy and gratitude that he shouted,

> Finally, when I visited the Zen master Ju-ching on Mt. T'ien-t'ung, the most important thing in my life, my search for the way, had ended.[2]

This statement is identical to Shinran's words:

> Even if I were to be deceived by Hōnen Shōnin, even if I were to fall into Hell because of saying the *nembutsu*, I would not regret it.[3]

Dōgen's expression "studying the Buddha's path" came out of this deep feeling toward his teacher.

When Rev. Akegarasu was a small child, his parents told him to visit Shinsen Kitakata, his relative and one of the greatest calligraphy masters in Kanazawa, to learn the art under him. When the master saw the boy, he told him, "There is no problem about giving you a model handwriting to copy. But I don't want to do that. You should learn your own handwriting." Thus Rev. Akegarasu did not have any formal training in calligraphy. The master's words contain a key that unlocks the secret of studying.

In studying predecessors' life-styles, we must ask, "What did they practice as the Buddha's path? Where did they seek the ideal?" They sought the ideal exclusively within themselves. They went deeper and deeper into themselves. In short, they sought the true self. The life-styles of all our predecessors show this.

Here, studying predecessors' life-styles must mean searching for the true self deep within ourselves. Studying predecessors suddenly turns into studying the self. Hereupon, the true model for the self is the self itself. When we attempt to learn from a predecessor, our hands, which cling to him, are cut off by him. We are severed from the predecessor by the predecessor himself. He shouts at us, "Stand alone!"

A typical samurai story goes like this: A young man enters the gate of a master swordsman in order to learn the martial art. But the master does not teach him the art at all. Instead of letting him hold a wooden sword, the teacher makes him do chores such as chopping wood, drawing water, and cleaning the house. In this way, three years pass. This story describes how the young man was pushed away by the master.

The real master does not guide the student by holding his hands, but pushes him away. He shouts at the student "Stand alone!" What must be studied is one's self. When the student comes to kneel before himself, the search for the self is over.

In short, the true predecessor is one's self. The true guide is my self. Thus studying the Buddha's path was actually studying the path of independence and freedom. It is studying the self, nothing else. The ultimate message of the Buddha's path is "Revere yourself!" The Buddha's path is a path that leads to independence and self-respect. This path cannot be understood by a person who slights the self.

People often confuse humility with low self-esteem. Having low self-esteem is a form of arrogance in which one makes a hasty conclusion about the self by underestimating it. It is the total opposite of humility. When one truly reveres and honors the self, he kneels before himself. This is an action of the utmost humility and selflessness.

With the words "studying the self," the Zen master describes the humblest path, on which one kneels before the self, considering it his teacher.

Here it has become clear that the "Buddha" in the term "Buddha's path" means *the true self*. Where should we seek a Buddha? Many people seek him outside themselves, considering him an external being that transcends them. But such a Buddha is an apparition. They are grasping a ghost. What is called the absolute one in false religions is precisely such a ghost. It is a product of the imagination; it does not *really exist*.

The "Buddha" is not the regular self that we consider the self; it is the true self that lies beyond the regular self—which is found when the regular self is transcended within us. To use Dr. Nishida's term, it is the self of "internal transcendence."[4] This self alone truly exists. It is not a product of the imagination.

To make it easy to understand the relationship between the true self (or the self of internal transcendence) and the regular self, Shin Buddhism uses words such as "parent" or "mother." Dōgen also uses the expression "the great master Śākyamuni Buddha who is a *compassionate father*" in the volume called *Gyōji* (Continuous Practice). These terms are designed to show that "Buddha" does not exist outside us as a being that transcends us externally.

The expression "studying the self" beautifully depicts the self's action in kneeling before the self. The true learner must kneel before that from which he is learning. Here the [learning] self is being nullified by the true self [which is being studied]. Here not a speck of selfness is found. The expression well describes the process: after selfness is totally wiped away before the true self, one stands as he is, as the true self. To rephrase, it shows that only the humblest person can be an independent person.

If someone says that although he can bow his head before others, he cannot do so before himself, he is a liar. If he cannot bow his head before himself, how could he do so before others? Being able to bow one's head before all existing things and being able to do so before oneself are one and the same thing. In this sense I say that studying the self is the humblest action.

It is in studying the self, however, that the path of independence, or the path of freedom, exists. The selfless person alone can regard the life of this world as his own life. He alone can live in a world where nothing stands against him.

Studying the self describes not only a life of inviolable independence and freedom, in which one realizes the true self in an inconceivable manner, but also the greatest humility, where not a speck of selfness is found.

Thus we can say that studying the self alone can fully and straightforwardly explain studying the Buddha's path.

Studying the Buddha's path means studying the path of the clearest *self-awakening*. Because it is a path of self-awakening, Buddhism can be differentiated sharply from false religions. The so-called false religions do not focus on self-awakening or introspection.

(3/1, 1955)

19

On History

The word history implies that a person can exist as a human being only when he learns. If the word history does not mean learning, it is quite useless to talk about it.

The basic meaning of history is that it is the history of learners. For example, it was only after Śākyamuni and Jesus thoroughly studied the Indian and Jewish spiritual cultures, respectively, that their spirits were reborn and they created new spiritual cultures.

Here human beings are basically presupposed to be "all [foolish] ordinary persons" [in the words of Prince Shōtoku].[1] The works of geniuses could not exist apart from history. Geniuses are geniuses because they learn from preceding history, because they are taught by it. Their learner's spirit is based upon their awareness that they are all [foolish] ordinary persons.

A person's self-awakening, that is, his awakening to the reality of the self, is also historical. I call it historical because his predecessors taught him how to examine himself and because he, on the basis of what he has learned, is going to open up a new future for himself. This is exactly what Dr. Nishida called "producing while being produced."[2]

It is only after a great man has thoroughly learned from previous history that he experiences self-awakening. Those who cannot thoroughly learn from previous history are little people. That is why I define a great man as a person who can make continuous effort in learning.

History generates and gives birth to great men. Thus a great man and his time are deeply connected. This is so because he is a learner. It is only by discovering the same awakening experience in his preceding culture, among his predecessors, that his awakening gradually matures, becomes enriched and perfected. The little people—those who do not know how to learn—do not know how to receive teachings from their predecessors or how to bow their heads humbly before them. Therefore they cannot deepen their awakening. They cannot open a new historical path.

My predecessors and I are all [foolish] ordinary persons. Thus their awakening could be identical to my awakening. My awakening could be identical to their awakening. If Śākyamuni and I had not been all [foolish] ordinary persons, I could not learn from him and he could not teach me. The term [foolish] ordinary persons means that we are all human beings.

It is not until a person thoroughly learns from his predecessors that his new world is created in his present historical context. Thus learning and creativity are one and the same.

In his *Tsurezure-gusa* (Reflections in Hours of Idleness), Kenkō Yoshida [1283–1350, a Japanese essayist] said, "Just as a person who imitates an insane person is insane, so a person who imitates a Buddha is also a Buddha."[3] I think his words are quite meaningful. Learning (*manabu*) must mean imitating (*maneru*). We can imitate our predecessors, we can copy their ways of acting and thinking, because we and they are all [foolish] ordinary persons. It is by the process of imitation that awakening arises in us. It is in this process of identifying ourselves with our predecessors that learning can take place.

And importantly, what is at issue here is *my* awakening. *My* awakening can only be historical. Since awakening inherently contains a transcendental quality, which works through imitating, we can transcend our predecessors while learning from them. This is true learning. That is why I say that learning and creativity are one and the same.

Historical creativity cannot take any other form than thoroughly learning from one's predecessors and eventually going beyond them. I have already said that it was not until Śākyamuni and Jesus learned from their preceding cultures that their new, creative, genius personalities were born. It was the same with Prince Shōtoku, Shinran, and Dōgen. Prince Shōtoku's *Sankyō-gisho* (Commentary on the Three Sutras) is nothing but a footstep that shows how seriously he learned. Shinran's *Kyōgyōshinshō* and Dōgen's *Shōbō-genzō* are the same. What would remain of those individuals if we eliminated their learning from their predecessors? Prince Shōtoku chose to learn from three sūtras, the *Lotus Sutra*, the *Vimalakīrti-nirdeśa-sūtra*, and the *Śrīmālādevī-siṃhanāda-sūtra*. Shinran chose the Pure Land tradition. Dōgen chose the Zen masters in China. Although the learning of all these individuals was limited in scope, they all thoroughly learned from their respective traditions.

The fact that a person's scope of learning is limited is inevitable, because each person's karmic conditions are specific and limited. Shinran, for example, considered the seven monks Nāgārjuna, Vasubandhu, T'an-luan, Tao-ch'o, Shan-tao, Genshin, and Hōnen his main predecessors.

How deeply Shinran bowed before his personal teacher Hōnen! How deeply Dōgen bowed before his personal teacher Ju-ching! They had nothing except their learning from their teachers. Learning the Dharma is the only concern in the mind of Prince Shōtoku, Shinran, and Dōgen.

It was out of their learning that their historical creativity was born. They knew their predecessors' teachings inside out and made free use of them. For example, Shinran's predecessors formed the world of his awakening. And he, having totally embraced those predecessors, stood up in his own awakening as an independent personality. The seven monks were instrumental only in realizing Shinran's unique personality and awakening. Shinran just developed his own awakening through (or by making use of) those seven monks. Here, because of the transcendental quality of awakening, Shinran and the seven monks exchanged places. The roles of servant and master were reversed. Shinran, having thoroughly learned from his Pure Land predecessors and gone beyond them, developed his own unique world of awakening. Dōgen was the same. Neither followed his predecessors blindly. However, they kept on learning from their teachers endlessly. Without this kind of historicity these three great individuals in Japanese history could not have existed.

By the term historicity I mean this: first, one learns as much as possible from his preceding culture and predecessors, and simultaneously transcends them because of the transcendental quality contained in self-awakening. Finally one opens up a new, unique sphere. Historicity is this creative action.

Learning does not mean blindly following. Learning is deeply connected with self-awakening. Since the transcendental quality contained in self-awakening works in learning, learning is precisely becoming independent.

Thus the person who does not know learning will never be independent. He will just maintain his self-assertion and self-affirmation; he will just keep on clashing with others because of his relative, competitive, posture.

In true learning one is selfless. In this selflessness, an independent world of awakening where one can become a unique expression of the world comes to be realized. This is the deep meaning of human historicity.

(2/20, 1965)

20

Learn Freedom!

Freedom is the ultimate goal of human beings. Could they have any higher goal? The dignity of the human spirit is freedom. We speak of people seeking salvation, but could there be any salvation greater than being free?

Freedom, however, should not be a freedom based on affirmation of the self. If a person affirms the self, he cannot be free because he is always restrained by the self. Freedom must be the freedom of nothingness, the freedom of selflessness. In other words, freedom exists only for the person who kneels down, because self-awakening [which is the basis of freedom] exists only when one experiences self-negation.

What, then, is this self-negation? To use everyday language, it is to be modest. It is to listen to others selflessly without asserting oneself.

Lenin said, "Take one step forward and two steps back!" Taking one step forward means asking questions, or knocking on the door of other people's minds. When other people start to speak, we should retreat and listen quietly and carefully. This thorough listening is taking two steps back. Further, we must think about what we have heard; over and over again we must ask the same questions in our own minds.

Thus one step of the two steps back is listening and the other step is thinking about what we have heard. Because we must both listen and think, we say to take two steps back.

Conversely, it is absolutely necessary for us to take two steps back in order to take one step forward. Taking two steps back means good learning. Good learning can make us take a creative step forward. Without good learning, without taking two steps back, we cannot take a creative step forward. If we only think about advancing, we will stumble and fall down. We cannot possibly take a firm, creative, steady step forward.

Taking two steps back means learning the words of our predecessors. The Zen master Dōgen said, "One should learn the regression in which one sends illumination backward to oneself."[1] A person who experiences self-awakening has the attitude of a learner. Quiet listening and careful thinking about what one has heard is the only thing that can make a person take a creative first step without any effort. More emphasis should be placed on learning than on thinking new ideas. Creativity comes quite naturally out of learning.

True thinking must be based on listening. For example, Plato listened to Socrates; Aristotle listened to Plato. When one thinks without listening, one's thought will be abstract speculation; it will go around and around and get nowhere. Thus the true human spirit can exist only in a specific historical context. Śākyamuni could not have attained his unique religious thought without listening to ancient Indian thought, particularly to the Vedas and the Upaniṣads. How could Jesus have attained his unique religious thought without listening to the religious ideas that his Jewish ancestors had handed down to him through the Old Testament? To state the point more accurately, human self-awakening is itself a historical matter.

Thus when one is listening to a predecessor's words, one is thinking within a historical context. Human thinking is impossible without words. Words—the heritage of a race and the carrier of all its traditional culture—are given to us by others. The fact that we can think only when a language is given to us by others means that our thinking is always historical thinking. We are made to think by words. The functioning of words inside us is called thinking. We do not so much think as we are made to think. This is the concrete aspect of the world of the human spirit. Our being made to think by words is called learning.

Śākyamuni was enabled to think by ancient Indian culture, by the Vedas and the Upaniṣads. Jesus was enabled to think by the Jewish ideas of the Old Testament. Christian scholars tell us that Jesus frequently used Old Testament terms in his sermons in the New Testament. Listening to a traditional culture and thereby being made to think in a historical context is called learning.

We must think about individuals such as Śākyamuni and Jesus. Without entertaining a deep adoration for those teachers, a feeling like love, we cannot possibly experience self-awakening. The world of the human spirit cannot be established.

What, then, should we think about and adore? Only one thing: our predecessors' personal freedom. For the world of the human spirit simply means the world of freedom. We must sincerely listen to and think about our predecessors' paths to freedom. Of course, real freedom exists in a sphere beyond thinking. But the path that leads to real freedom is the path of thinking. We must follow it through and through. And we must listen. Listening means thinking. The path that leads to freedom is thinking. But if we are attached to the path of thinking, we do not have freedom. When we attain freedom, thinking, too, must be abandoned. When we exhaust thinking and then go beyond it, we have freedom.

Those who desire to reach freedom must not be afraid of thinking. For example, when Śākyamuni was sitting under the Bodhi Tree, his mind was not void of thoughts. He had engaged in ascetic practices in a forest for six years before he meditated under the tree. During those six years he thought deeply. And finally, under the Bodhi Tree at Buddha Gaya, he abandoned the thinking to which he had devoted his entire being for six years. He was liberated from it. Although he was liberated from it, the path that led him to freedom was nothing but thinking.

We cannot intuit freedom abruptly, without listening and thinking. The world of the human spirit exists only in a historical context. We can experience genuine self-awakening only in a historical context. Thus we must listen and think to the best of our ability. We must know that intuition exists only when our thinking reaches its limit.

Shinran exhausted thinking in his *Kyōgyōshinshō*. Who could say that this text is not the product of his thought? The Zen master Dōgen did the same thing in his *Shōbō-genzō*. Those who fear and evade thinking cannot arrive at freedom because they neglect listening. If we do not thoroughly travel the path of thinking, it is impossible for us to get to freedom.

When I use expressions like "the human spirit" or "the world of the human spirit," I am focusing on the idea of freedom. I am exclusively emphasizing the importance of freedom, the actualization or fulfillment of freedom in our lives. When I mention that we must thoroughly study a tradition, I am saying that we must concentrate our attention on only one thing—freedom. We must ask if a certain person has freedom. If he has it, we learn about it, we learn the path leading to it. I am not talking about learning that does not have any clear focus.

For example, we must ask whether Śākyamuni had freedom. We must think deeply about this. If we discover freedom in a person, we must learn all about it by exhausting our thinking within a historical context.

Our intuition will sharply tell us whether a certain person has freedom or not. Why did Shinran go to Hōnen? How did the Zen master Dōgen find the Zen master Ju-ching? They must have intuited freedom with the totality of their beings.

When Shinran was on Mt. Hiei, how much he struggled and questioned whether he should go down the mountain and under whom he should study! When he attempted a hundred-day meditation in Rokkakudō Hall, he was about to make a final decision as to whom he was going to study under.

The Zen master Dōgen traveled to many places in the great Sung country. Having searched for a teacher under whom he could learn, he came to the conclusion that for him, there was no true teacher in China. Thus he decided to return to Japan and waited for a ship. Then he happened to see a Chinese monk who advised him to visit Mt. T'ien-t'ung to see a Zen master [i.e., Ju-ching].

Thus the searching eyes of these two individuals discovered and met with two of the most extraordinary teachers. Since human beings are made to seek freedom by their deepest reality, they inevitably search for freedom. They cannot help asking where among their predecessors they can find freedom. "Knock, and the door will open. Seek, and it will be given." Human beings can intuit whether a certain person has freedom or not. Thus this intuition for freedom guides one in the process of exhausting historical thinking in the sphere of the human spirit. Learning has a definite objective. The expression "exhaust learning" may give the impression that one is abandoned in an endlessly vast field where one cannot find any trail. But it is not that kind of learning. If one sincerely yearns for freedom, one will certainly meet with a teacher.

Learning, or exhausting thinking within a historical context, does not mean that one looks at the spiritual teachers of the world and vaguely wonders under whom one should study. It means that one actually meets with a teacher—an event totally determined by one's karmic conditions.

The most essential problem in the sphere of the human spirit is, after all, whether one meets with a teacher or not. The focal point is whether one meets with a real human being, a real personality. Specificity is so important in the sphere of the human spirit. Such a meeting happens in this actual world; it does not happen in the world of abstract concepts.

We must know that the Dharma[2] makes the world of the human spirit exist in this actual world. The world of the human spirit becomes reality when we meet with a real human being, a human being who breathes real air in the real world. And the crucial issue is whether or not we, by meeting with such a real human being, experience self-awakening. This is a down-to-earth matter.

The Dharma makes the world of the human spirit exist. It is not an abstract matter. It is a matter of bloody karmic conditions in the actual world. It is in this context that we meet with a real personality, a free human being.

After meeting this real human being, we can only exhaust thinking within a historical context. For example, Shinran could not help doing so after he met his teacher Hōnen. Dōgen was the same when he met his teacher Ju-ching. Both wholeheartedly and desperately studied and studied; they exhausted thinking within a historical context. And they fully experienced the highest form of freedom attainable by human beings.

These free teachers were men of compassion. They kindly revealed to us a life of compassion that has everlasting significance for our lives. We can vividly see in them, in actual historical individuals, what the world of the human spirit is all about.

The only thing we must do is to learn limitlessly, forever. In learning, we experience tremendous joy. That is why we must learn endlessly and limitlessly. And the Dharma is this limitlessness. It is "the perpetual learning of the Bodhisattva Dharmākara" [which is mentioned in the *Larger Sukhāvatīvyūha-sūtra*]. The Buddha Lokeśvararāja teaches Dharmākara that he can eventually attain the goal of awakening if he keeps on learning endlessly, just as a determined person could empty an ocean with a ladle.[3] After receiving this teaching, Dharmākara starts his perpetual learning. What a joy it is! If our learning had an end, how miserable it would be! Indeed, the end of learning means death. There can be no death in the Dharma. Because of his perpetual learning, that is, as soon as he makes up his mind to keep on learning forever, Dharmākara becomes a Buddha by the name of Limitless Life (*Amitāyus*). When he determines to learn limitlessly because of his limitless ignorance, the Buddha named Limitless Life is born.

There can be no end to live human thinking or to thinking within a historical context. Real, live thinking must take the form of perpetual learning. The deathless life is a life of limitless searching. As soon as one says to oneself, "I've got it," one dies. One must say to oneself, "Today I have learned this much. What new things will I learn tomorrow?" and go to bed with a delightful anticipation of the next day's learning. There can be no actualization of Limitless Life in our lives apart from this. Facing an unknown future, we, here and now, engage in learning to the best of our ability. What greater life could we have?

Actually, we know nothing. We exist here and now but do not know the limitless future. We are limitlessly ignorant. And it is because of our ignorance that we desire to learn. As we face the new, limitless, and creative development of eternal life, we live our inconceivable present life—inconceivable because of our ignorance. This is how all human beings without exception exist.

The expression "I Bow to the Tathāgata of Inconceivable Light"[4] means that the unknown future is developing limitlessly, here and now, moment after moment. It also means that I, a totally ignorant one, live, or more accurately, am made to live, by kneeling before this inconceivable constant development. Here my life is one with limitless life, with the Dharma of impermanence. It is being permeated by it. Because of my ignorance, I just entrust my entire being to the limitless development of the Dharma. This is my life, my life that is permeated by the Dharma.

"My learning" and "my ignorance" are synonyms. Because of my ignorance everything is new and fresh. Life is fresh moment after moment. New, creative life is given exclusively to ignorant persons. For me, facing eternal life means that I touch its limitless newness with my totally ignorant self. There is no other way to intuit eternal life. The indispensable condition for intuiting it is my total ignorance here and now.

Thus learning or searching is the only important thing in my life. I constantly experience surprise and wonder. There is always fresh life. I constantly meet with a new and rare phase of life that I have not encountered before.

One who experiences joy through touching upon such a life will not forget the joy. Since this constantly creative life gives him new joy day after day, he cannot stop living the life of a seeker.

He lives only as a learner. He is not at all interested in wearing the facial expression of a knowing person, or in coming up with any conclusions. He is not at all interested in saying (or listening to) any definitive ideas. Just like a newborn baby, he enjoys the fresh, limitless wonder of this present world. There he experiences the moment-by-moment birth and newness of life.

"One's old life dies and one is reborn into a new life"—this should not be a mere expression, but a personal experience filled with the same feeling of surprise and wonder that is found in the birth of a baby. My becoming a totally ignorant person is my death in this present moment. It is only when I become a totally ignorant person that the new moment-by-moment development of the Dharma is revealed to me. What fresh joy is given to a person who has died in his ignorance!

Thus when I joyfully become one with the new development of the Dharma, I am living the Dharma. The life of a learner is the only way of living the Dharma. There is no way to become one with the Dharma apart from learning. The most important essence of the human spirit is learning, because only learning can make us go back to the Dharma. Freedom can be experienced in learning. A real learner is a man of freedom. He is also a man permeated by the Dharma.

(3/6, 1965)

PART THREE

The Teachings of Rev. Akegarasu

21

Symphony of the Flame

1

Here in Ishikawa Prefecture we have two great modern thinkers. One is Dr. Kitarō Nishida, and the other is the Rev. Haya Akegarasu. I am deeply grateful for the good fortune of having been taught by both of them. Dr. Nishida taught me while I was studying philosophy at the University of Kyoto, and Rev. Akegarasu is still teaching me by admonishing me. On this radio program, I would like to talk about what kind of teaching I have been receiving from Rev. Akegarasu.

Rev. Akegarasu is now seventy-six years old. What has he taught us during his life? I believe that the people of Ishikawa Prefecture must know. What is the central point in his thought? If we were to pick one crucial sentence out of his writing, out of his life, what would it be?

So far Rev. Akegarasu has written over a hundred books. From these voluminous writings I would like to point out the one sentence which clearly represents his spirit. In my opinion, this sentence can be found in his most important work, *Trilogy of Rebirth* (which consists of *Before and After Rebirth*, *Declaration of an Independent Person*, and *The Advancing One*)[1]:

> The flame from the cremation of my entire self is my only
> liberation.[2]
>
> (*Declaration of an Independent Person*)

The entire self is to be burned up, cremated; then there will be flames coming out of the burning self. He says that this flame, this fiercely burning flame, is his only liberation. I believe that this statement sums up his entire life and expresses the core of his thought.

Does the sentence really reflect, as I think, the entire life of Rev. Akegarasu and his deepest thought? The idea must be fully examined. If my view is based on my arbitrary, subjective opinion, it has no value. So I must examine objectively whether the sentence truly represents Rev. Akegarasu's life or not.

Now I will, by explaining what the sentence means, attempt to show what I have been learning from Rev. Akegarasu. I will attempt to explain that in the last analysis, learning from him means learning from this sentence. I will also reveal what kind of person I am. I sincerely hope that my listeners will correct my misunderstandings.

First, I must explain Rev. Akegarasu's statement. He is saying that his entire self is perishing. It is important to note that all of his self is negated and destroyed, not only a part of it. The crucial point is that the self no longer exists. This is expressed in his use of the term "entire." He is not negating a part of his self, saying, "This is a bad part of myself," or "I have this or that shortcoming." If he did so, the self which is reflecting upon itself would still be there. The complaining self, which is looking at the shortcomings of the self, would still be there. Instead, Rev. Akegarasu says "entire"; he throws away all of himself. This is not a matter of the good self or the bad self. All of his self, with both the good and the bad parts of it, is cast away.

I will give two examples. Suppose that there is a picture, a masterpiece by Taikan Yokoyama [1868–1958, a Japanese painter]. Someone comes to this picture and smears it with a drop of ink. It is true that the place he ruined is only a little portion of the entire work, but we must say that the whole picture is ruined.

Or suppose that you have a toothache. Although the tooth is only a small part of your body, your entire being experiences the pain. You cannot smile and say, "Well, my tooth is in pain." Your entire being experiences the pain and suffering.

Similarly, if one part of the self is defiled, all of it is defiled. Partial contamination is total contamination. If a part of the self contains a little bit of badness or corruption, the self as a whole is bad and corrupted. That is why the teacher throws away all of himself.

Here Rev. Akegarasu is not trusting his self. He never believes that there is anything good about himself. He abandons himself as being a totally useless and incompetent person, as being good for nothing. He never even dreams that he will be capable of doing something good in this world; he does not have any faith in his own power or ability. He gives up attachment to himself and believes that his whole self might as well be abandoned—that it should be sent to a crematorium. He is saying that such a self does not deserve to live.

"Cremation of my entire self" is the teacher's confession. It shows his awakening to the fact that "Hell is my only home."[3] It expresses his realization that he, a totally good-for-nothing being, is simply creating problems in this world—that he is trash, the worst of all evildoers. This is the painful, heartfelt confession of a person who has found that he does not deserve to live. A dead body will decay. But he discovered that his self, though living, was already decaying. It was "a living corpse." Such a decaying thing, he believes, might as well be burned in order to create purity in this world.

In this statement of Rev. Akegarasu's, there is neither ambition to achieve anything in this world nor pride in his own ability, talents, and intelligence. Napoleon once said that there was no such word as "impossible" in his dictionary. But in the teacher's dictionary there is only one word: "impossible." Here the teacher has been completely disappointed in his own ability, or rather in his very self. "Cremation of my entire self" is his shout of despair. A person who has not bumped into this dazzling wall of impossibility and despair will never have the chance to enter into the Absolute World. Despair is the door to religion. Which of us do not experience despair when we really think about ourselves, when we deeply examine ourselves?

2

When we are totally disappointed in the self, when the self has been abandoned as something completely useless and incapable, the entire self is sent to a crematorium and burned as a living corpse. Flames flare up from the burning corpse. Compare this flame with the decayed corpse, the decayed self. How beautiful the flame is! But the fuel for this beautiful flame is that very defiled self. This flame shoots forth many radiant colors: red, white, yellow, green, and purple. We are enchanted by the beauty of the flame, even though it is burning up our selves.

There are many flames in this world. But no other flame is so strong, sharp, and refreshing as this flame which burns up the self. Its incredible beauty penetrates into the depth of our guts. Even while we are being burned up, we cannot help admiring and praising its beauty. How inconceivable this is! Yet we experience this kind of thing in life. For example, we say, "Even though he is my enemy, I admire him." If our enemy defeats us in a truly beautiful manner, we cannot help admiring his victory and forgetting our defeat. Another example is falling in love. When we are overwhelmed and enchanted by a person's charm, we lose ourselves in admiring the person. Falling in love means having our soul completely taken away by the other. What is this but perfect defeat? But it is a refreshing and joyful defeat, very different from a defeat of the usual kind. Similarly, the flame which burns up all of the corrupted self is magnificently solemn, refreshing, and beautiful.

What, then, is the essence of the fire that burns us up? The ancient Greek philosopher Heracleitus said, "The universe is a mass of burning fire, and it does not keep the same shape even for a second. It is constantly changing." He expressed the same idea by saying *panta rhei* (everything flows). In other words, Heracleitus expressed the truth that everything in this world is impermanent by using the symbol of fire. Heracleitus makes me realize that the flame in the teacher's statement refers to the truth of impermanence.

The truth of impermanence, the tremendous flow of universal life, washes away this petty self of ours, this self that is always saying, "I am good, I am bad, I am dependable, I am undependable." All our endeavors are inundated and absorbed into the powerful flow. This flame is the eternal flow of universal life. It makes us realize that we, not perceiving the existence of that great universal life, have contracted ourselves into the tiny shell of the self, saying, "I am good, I am bad, I am capable, I am incapable." Illumined by the truth of impermanence, by the truth of the infinite, absolute, eternal flow of life, we come to recognize the finiteness and relativity of the self. This recognition is "the cremation of my entire self." This is nothing but our recognition of the true nature of the self, a recognition that takes place when we are illumined by the light of the flame, the light of truth and wisdom.

"The flame from the cremation" means the flame of the universe itself, not the little flame that the petty self makes. It is the eternal life of the universe. It is also the truth to which the Tathāgata is awakened. In this sense the flame refers to Limitless Life and Limitless Light. The cremation of my entire self does not mean that we are burning the self; it refers to *our being burned* by the fire of impermanence, by universal life itself. It refers to *our being made to know* the true— finite and limited—nature of the self when we are illumined by the light of the truth of impermanence. This is the true meaning of "the cremation of my entire self."

Thus the flame refers to something entirely beyond the power of the self. It is the fire of the Tathāgata, not our fire. It is not until we meet with the light, wisdom, and truth of the Tathāgata that we come to recognize the futility of the self. Earlier I said that "the cremation of my entire self" is the teacher's confession. It is not a confession that he makes on his own; it is a confession that he is made to make through his encounter with the wisdom of the Tathāgata. It is because of the existence of the fire, the absolute fire, that the self is burned. The fire exists first; our cremation takes place later.

Therefore, Rev. Akegarasu forgets himself in praising the fire of the universe (i.e., the life and wisdom of the Tathāgata) that burns up all of his petty self. There is nothing left but a mass of flame. As Heracleitus said, the only reality is fire. In other words, Rev. Akegarasu understands the truth of impermanence. In Buddhism, "wisdom" refers to insight into the truth of impermanence. Here the teacher is praising and venerating this truth. His confession of the self's futility is his praise of the Tathāgata; his veneration of the flame is the cremation of the self. Confession is praise and praise is confession. In the statement we hear, directly from Rev. Akegarasu, Shan-tao's words—"The Name-saying [i.e., the *nembutsu*] that I perform moment after moment is my constant confession."[4] Rev. Akegarasu forgets himself in praising the fire of the universe. It is the very reality of the fire, or his insight into the truth of impermanence, that makes him forget himself.

Buddhism talks about selflessness. But the teacher does not have to force himself to be selfless. Instead, he is living a peaceful, selfless life quite naturally, forgetting the self in recognizing and praising the flame as the only reality. The universal fire that burns up the entire self is the voice of wisdom, which is described [in the *Larger Sukhāvatīvyūha-sūtra*]: "The great voice of the Truly Awakened One resonates throughout the ten directions."[5] I cannot help visualizing Rev. Akegarasu quietly listening to the voice. The sound of impermanence is playing an exquisite symphony. I cannot help calling it the symphony of the flame. It is in listening to this symphony that Rev. Akegarasu says he experiences his only liberation.

It is when his finite and limited self is absorbed into the eternal flow of universal life that the teacher experiences liberation. For him, the symphony of the flame, or, more accurately, listening to the symphony of the flame, was the only path to liberation. To use a philosophical expression, his liberation consisted of seeing and recognizing impermanence, which is the only truth, the most fundamental Dharma in the world. It consisted of *being illumined* by the light of this truth.

3

Rev. Akegarasu says that the flame itself is his liberation. This means that recognizing the truth of impermanence is his liberation; there is no other.

What, then, is liberation? Liberation exists only for the person who has been disappointed in his self. As long as we depend even a little bit upon the self's abilities and believe that we can accomplish something, the word "liberation" means nothing to us. It is not until we give up, recognize the impossibility of controlling ourselves, and throw the self away that liberation becomes real for the first time. Only when a person sees the futility of his entire being does he truly seek liberation. Therefore liberation is a matter of humility. Liberation becomes real only for the person who has painfully realized that his self is good for nothing, unreliable, and incompetent; it cannot exist for a conceited person who relies upon his self.

Thus liberation is actualized through an absolute power beyond the self. Rev. Akegarasu discovered this absolute power beyond the self in the flame from the cremation of the entire self; flame is a symbol for a power beyond the self. But does liberation suggest weakness because it exists only for a totally incompetent person? At first sight it may seem so. On careful reflection, however, we realize that even what we consider the weak self has already been extinguished. The relative self that can be called weak or strong has already been nullified. The totality of the self has been absorbed into the flame that is the universe itself; there is not even a shadow of the self left. There are no longer such categories as weak or strong. The flame from the cremation of the entire self is beyond weak and strong. Only this flame is real; there is nothing else that can be compared to it. It is unique and absolute. When the self is swallowed up by the mass of universal flame and consumed by it, only this unique and absolute fire remains.

When we forget ourselves in praising the flame, when we become one with the flame, new selves arise. This transition must be experienced; logic cannot trace or explain it. In Greek mythology there is the story of the phoenix, which emerges, flapping its wings, from its own ashes. The phoenix explains my teacher's words. The bird rediscovers itself in the very midst of the flame which is burning it. We call this rebirth, spiritual revolution, revival, or new life. It is an actual experience of liberation. When the teacher says "my only liberation," he is talking about the inconceivable experience of rebirth and new life. It is a *unique* and *absolute* experience; no other experience in this world can be compared to it.

Here Rev. Akegarasu stands up. When we throw away all of the self as good for nothing, we merge into infinite, absolute life; we are born anew and stand up as naked human beings. We shout "In the heavens and on the earth, my aloneness is noble."[6] This is "the declaration of an independent person." A person who has already experienced this unique and absolute liberation stands up like this. There opens up for him a life, a path, in which he enjoys complete freedom without hindrance, without attachment or stagnation.

When the teacher says "The flame of the cremation ...," he is making an independent person's declaration that he has nothing to fear in this world. The petty self that competes with others has already died. It has been cremated. The liberated one is the one who has become one with the eternal life of the universe. It is the independent person, the naked human being himself. It is like a naive baby that smiles, cries, rejoices, and struggles. It is a human being who, without being attached to anything, thinks as his human nature dictates, speaks as he wishes, and acts as he feels like acting. It is a human being just as he is. I cannot describe the independent person in any other way. Being unafraid of anything means being unattached to anything. If the independent person feels weak, he just lives the life of a weak person. If he feels strong, he just lives the life of a strong person. His life is natural and spontaneous without any attachment, with nothing forced upon himself or others. His life is just as it is. It is flexible. The independent person is flexible. Rev. Akegarasu, whom we can see face to face, is flexibility itself. Nobody else has his naïveté, naturalness, and directness. He is an independent person, a free person, a person of flat-ordinariness.

What is the secret of the teacher's flexibility? He is flexible because he is living the truth of impermanence. Truly to penetrate the truth of impermanence means to live this truth, to become one with it. To be one with the truth of impermanence is to be flexible. However, we should not forget that to be one with the truth of impermanence is to be one with the burning flame. That is why we see before our eyes Rev. Akegarasu, untiringly learning and seeking the Dharma—just like a devouring fire. The fire of his spirit burns up everything it touches.

In Rev. Akegarasu, who does not spare his life in teaching the Dharma, we see the dignity of the independent person. Anyone who touches his spirit will find the courage to stand up. The secret of his infinite power, I believe, lies in this statement that I have been explaining. This secret is quite simple. He throws his petty self into the universal fire, the fire of universal life, and has it burned up by its flame. In other words, he throws his whole self into the flow of impermanence. Then, eternal life itself, not his own power, works in him. This is the secret of the teacher's power.

This power, however, does not belong to the teacher alone. All of us can certainly attain this power, if we, together with the teacher, have ourselves cremated and revere the fire that burns us up. No one is so strong as the person who has experienced this liberation. He is strong in the sense that he is beyond the relativity of strong and weak.

If liberation is the most important thing for us, then the teacher's statement brings good news. If liberation is the most crucial thing for the teacher and for the people of the world, I consider this the most important statement of Rev. Akegarasu's life.

My explanation of his statement has not been thorough. It may not have touched upon even the surface of his deep spirit. But I have attempted to explain that my selection of this sentence as the most important statement of his life is based not upon my subjective liking but rather upon objective reasons. This has also been my attempt to present my understanding of Buddhism. Now I hope that my listeners correct my inadequate explanation.

Be that as it may, this is how I understand the essence of Rev. Akegarasu's teaching. I just cannot help saying that all of the teaching I am receiving from him is summarized in that one expression. This is myself. And this is my Rev. Akegarasu.

22

The Crucial Essence of Shinshū

1

Hōnen wrote his *Senjaku-shū*[1] at the request of Zenjō Hiromutsu (also known as Tsukinowa-den Kanezane, whose Dharma name was Enshō). This text describes *the crucial essence of Shinshū*, or the deep meaning of the *nembutsu*. The reader can understand it easily. It is indeed the rarest and most superior of texts. It is the highest and deepest treasure in all literature.

(*Kyōgyōshinshō*, Epilogue[2])

This describes the manner in which Shinran regarded the main work of his teacher; it also describes the manner in which I regard the main work of my teacher, the Rev. Haya Akegarasu. Previously I extracted some articles from his writings and compiled and published them as the *Lion's Roar*.[3] The first chapter of that book is entitled "Śākyamuni's Exact Thought at the Moment of His Awakening." I recognize in it Rev. Akegarasu's one ultimate statement. This one ultimate statement describes his crucial essence of Shinshū.

The term *Shinshū* literally means the religion (*shū*) of truth (*shin*) or religion as truth itself. The crucial essence, in the final analysis, refers to one ultimate statement. What is the one ultimate statement of Rev. Akegarasu? He says,

In this sense, Śākyamuni's exact thought at the moment of his awakening was his realization that "I am the devil."[4]

This statement, "I am the devil," is Rev. Akegarasu's ultimate statement. Indeed, his whole understanding of Buddhism is in this one sentence. The totality of his grasp of Buddhism is encompassed in it. Throughout his life, he used millions of words to exalt Buddhism. But the final thing he wanted to say was nothing but this one sentence. It was the one thing he exalted and explained. For it was the exact thought of Śākyamuni at the moment of his awakening, without which there would be no Buddhism. If we miss this core, whatever we say has nothing to do with Buddhism.

Have people grasped Buddhism in this way? Have they reached this crucial core by writing their general outlines of Buddhism? It is in this one sentence that Rev. Akegarasu attained absolute freedom. His liberation was in this. He believed that Buddhist liberation exists only in this one sentence, nothing else.

"I am the devil" is a thought which does not retain even a fragment of good within the self. For example, Dr. Kitarō Nishida wrote *A Study of the Good*.[5] Investigation of the good is possible only if we presuppose the potentiality for good within ourselves. But how can we possibly study the good if we are not connected with the good at all, if we do not have any relationship with the good? Speaking more clearly, what happens if a devil studies the good? Something exactly like a ghost will appear.

2

From "I am the devil," no good whatsoever emerges. Evil is the only thing that comes out of it, continuously—there is no possibility at all of producing any kind of good through study of the good. Thus a person who knows he is a devil does not undertake the study of the good.

Dr. Nishida also wrote *Intuition and Reflection within the Context of Self-awakening*.[6] In this book he examined what he called human self-awakening. As a result of this examination, did he reach the realization that he is a devil? The answer is no. In my opinion, the only thing that should be called real human self-awakening is awakening to being a devil. Aside from this, there is no self-awakening worthy of the name. Whatever else is called self-awakening is shallow, superficial, and halfway; it does not reach the reality of the self at all. Thus it does not deserve the name of self-awakening. In that sense, what people in this world usually call self-awakening is not real self-awakening at all. Real self-awakening is awakening to being a devil.

Not a bit of self-affirmation comes out of such genuine self-awakening. No self-justification comes out of it. Dr. Nishida discusses self-awakening from various angles. In this he betrays the fact that he has not reached the final, decisive conclusion, the ultimate point in self-awakening. If he had touched upon this final point in self-awakening, the only self-awakening worthy of the name, he would not have written this kind of book! A person who has grasped the final, uniquely genuine self-awakening does not engage in that type of "detailed, complicated, and roundabout" (*hansa*) speculation, but regards it as nonsense.

Everything discussed by Dr. Nishida in that book is false, because the self-awakening that is most crucial to him is not a unique, genuine one. The "intuition" and "reflection" that he discusses in the context of it are totally false. This is quite natural, because his self-awakening is not a true one. So the book as a whole is nothing but a book of lies. How impossible it is for a person to grasp truth when he assumes academic postures, such as that of philosophy!

Genuine self-awakening is given to us only in religion. The same thing can be said about truth itself. When I say things like this, scholars consider me dogmatic. On the contrary, it is the scholars who are standing on a dogma—the dogma that it is possible for something good or just to come out of the self. "I am the devil" smashes to pieces the dogma of scholars—their academic stance. If dogma is self-affirmation, "I am the devil" leaves no room at all for self-affirmation.

3

Truth cannot be grasped in a complicated and roundabout manner. As long as there is complicated investigation, dogma and self-affirmation are presupposed. Truth must be grasped without presuppositions. This grasping is always intuitive. Thus truth is grasped through intuition, not through complexity. Let me give you an example. Prince Shōtoku reacts to Fa-yüan's *Commentary on the Lotus Sutra* as follows:

> The interpreter's [Fa-yüan's] comment on this section of the sūtra is too subtle and fine, too bothersome and extensive. My foolish mind cannot understand it. Therefore I will not discuss it in full. I will leave it unexplained.[7]

Here, "subtle and fine" means the above-mentioned "detailed," and "bothersome and extensive" means "complicated and roundabout." Prince Shōtoku cut off these problems with the sharp statement "my foolish mind cannot understand it." It is, however, in this very statement that truth, intuition of truth, exists. If it had not been for this truth, the falsity of what is subtle, fine, bothersome, and extensive would not have been cut off.

Truth is simple. "I will not discuss it in full" cuts off and abandons. "I will leave it unexplained" means that it is not necessary to dwell upon falsity. The person with a foolish mind cannot investigate and examine truth. He cannot write a treatise on it. "My foolish mind cannot understand it" is talking about intuition itself, intuition of truth. It is certainly simple.

Let me cite another example. The *Records of the Dharma Talks of Hyakujō* [henceforth abbreviated as the *Records*] says,

> I am the only evil person in this world. In going to Hell, I am alone. In going to the Pure Land, I am alone. I have awakened to the fact that I am completely alone in everything.[8]

It is totally impossible for Dante (in his *Divine Comedy*) to enter the world of this truth. The whole *Divine Comedy* is only an expression of falsity. Just as Prince Shōtoku cut off, with one phrase of truth, Fa-yüan's *Commentary on the Lotus Sutra*, this passage in the *Records* cuts off Dante's lifework. Dante travels through Hell with Virgil, his guide. Dante is, as it were, sightseeing as other people fall into Hell. But there is actually no such Hell. Such a Hell is unreal, because the real Hell is one which Dante falls into all by himself. Both the

Purgatory and the Heaven that are developed on the basis of his false description of Hell are also nothing but falsity. In short, the whole *Divine Comedy* is an expression of falsity. Moreover, we should note that not a fragment of Christianity, not a fragment of religion, is described in it. Many Westerners regard it as one of the most important works in the world because they do not know what truth is. There cannot be real truth aside from religious truth. Westerners honor this book because they do not know religious truth. In the above passage in the *Records*, our unknown ancestor clearly states religious truth. With it he kicks the "subtle, fine, bothersome, and extensive" *Divine Comedy* into the Hell of falsity. I must say that this passage has the formidable power of truth.

4

Statements like this one in the *Records* are the language of the purest essence of self-awakening. They describe self-awakening so clearly that Dr. Nishida's *Intuition and Reflection within the Context of Self-awakening* cannot be compared with them. It does not dare to approach them out of shame. If Dr. Nishida had really understood such statements, he would not have undertaken such a roundabout discussion of self-awakening. The same thing can be said of his *A Study of the Good*.

Now let me comment on each sentence in the above passage. "I am the only evil person in this world"—this is a shout of thoroughgoing self-awakening. Where, in the above-mentioned two works of Dr. Nishida's, can we hear it? We are simply surprised by the roundaboutness of so-called scholars. The fact that real self-awakening is expressed in a passage by an unknown person indicates that real truth is not academic truth. It is religious truth, which foolish, ignorant, and ordinary people understand through their intuition. Bear in mind that the deepest truth cannot be grasped by scholars; but it can be clearly recognized by ordinary people in their self-awakening.

"In going to Hell, I am alone"—this means that only Hell comes out of the self. If the self creates a world, that world is only Hell. Not a bit of good emerges from the self. For such a self, writing texts like

A Study of the Good is totally unimaginable. The self cannot benefit this world. It is nothing but a hunk of evil. There is nothing in it but suffering. Its reality can only be described as a solitary fall into Hell.

This reality, all of a sudden, turns out to be life in the Pure Land. It instantly changes into a life of absolute freedom. Such a transformation is described in the statement "In going to the Pure Land, I am alone." This solitary going to Hell *is simultaneously* a solitary going to the Pure Land. This "*is simultaneously*" connotes a sudden transformation. The thorough liquidation of self-affirmation, in which not the least bit of one's goodness or justness is affirmed, is the absolute freedom of selflessness. At the end of his *Intuition and Reflection within the Context of Self-awakening*, Dr. Nishida arrived at what he called "the will of absolute freedom." But is this identical with the absolute freedom of selflessness (as described in the statement, "In going to the Pure Land, I am alone")—which resulted from the destruction of the self (as described in the statement, "In going to Hell, I am alone")? No, because Dr. Nishida did not fully grasp the unique and genuine self-awakening of "In going to Hell, I am alone."

"I have awakened to the fact that I am completely alone in everything"; here the world of aloneness is established. "Completely alone" is indeed not complicated. When we concern ourselves about the business of others, this world becomes difficult, complicated, entangled, bothersome, and sticky. The world of complete aloneness, in which one is not concerned about others, is extremely simple. The author of the *Records* clarifies in this last line the simplicity of human self-awakening. This is the simplicity, the thoroughness, of self-awakening—of looking into the self alone.

5

When the self alone is being examined, self-awakening becomes simple and thorough. Real self-awakening must concern the self *alone*. The thoroughness that comes out of this self-awakening enables us to grasp truth, which is simple. When Prince Shōtoku says that his foolish mind cannot understand it, it is quite clear that this statement concerns only one individual—Prince Shōtoku himself, no one else. Thus real self-awakening is simple. In saying "I have awakened to the fact that I am completely alone in everything," the author of the *Records*, too, indicates that he is referring to himself alone. This sentence further indicates that truth exists only in the world of self-awakening. "Everything" means all things—all phenomena, all matters, and all affairs. It refers to everything in this world. The fact that "everything" exists only in the world of self-awakening means that the truth can be recognized only subjectively in the sphere of self-awakening, of introspection.

Indeed, truth is not perfectly recognized unless it is recognized subjectively in the sphere of self-awakening. Truth must be something that encompasses the recognizer of truth, that makes the recognizer exist, and that makes recognition itself exist.

For example, the realization that one is the devil is dynamic indeed. One cannot stay there. The dynamism of this self-awakening is transition, impermanence. In "I am the devil," the truth of impermanence is grasped subjectively—precisely as a self-awakening process.

Self-awakening is itself impermanence. In it, truth and recognition of truth are one. It is there that truth is recognized concretely.

This dynamism arises moment after moment in the self alone. It is clear to everyone that the self does not stay the same even for a second. If we look at external things in an objective manner, we may see them as static. But when we look into the self, we see nothing static there. That is why I say that the truth of impermanence is grasped in the process of self-understanding itself. Or, more accurately, the truth of impermanence clearly manifests itself only in the process of self-awakening. Only in self-awakening can men truly grasp impermanence.

To speak in extremes: Only self-awakening IS impermanence. Impermanence is self-awakening. We must know why truth is self-awakening. When we speak of self-awakening, truth is always at issue. Moreover, truth must be seen in it in a concrete form. Rev. Akegarasu has shown the truth of impermanence in a concrete form—precisely by saying, "I am the devil." I said earlier that one cannot stay in the realization that one is the devil, because the self is already destroyed and smashed to pieces by it.

6

Since one is smashed to pieces, one cannot remain the same self any longer. This is the dynamic phase of self-awakening. While being smashed to pieces, the self, which cannot stay in the state of being a devil, immediately attains rebirth—like a phoenix that revives and flaps its wings. One is reborn into a new life. This is a life of perfect freedom. This is the highest point in dynamism. This is the life that nothing can hinder. It is not until we attain this life of perfect freedom that we are living truth, the truth of impermanence. Without such freedom we cannot truly (i.e., in an *an und für sich* manner) live impermanence. When a person whose self (*an sich*) exists as impermanence, and who is made to exist by impermanence, lives impermanence in his self-awakening, he attains a life of perfect freedom. A life in which he is one with impermanence in his self-awakening (i.e., in an *an und für sich* manner) is a life of perfect freedom.

The secret of human freedom lies in "I am the devil." It lies in "I am the only evil person in this world." Only religion shows the way to freedom. No matter how logically one may define freedom in terms of ethics and morals, there cannot be real freedom there. It is only in total liquidation of the self, i.e., in religious selflessness, that real human freedom can be experienced.

Being free means living the truth. Living the truth is made possible by recognition of the truth. This means that one must first understand the self. It is only through self-awakening that the truth is grasped. Or it should be said that self-awakening is itself truth. When one truly understands oneself, one becomes free.

There is no way to freedom except self-awakening. Such self-awakening is expressed by "I am the devil" or by "I am the only evil person in this world."

Let me give another example to clarify the way from self-awakening to freedom. Genshin [942–1017, the sixth patriarch of Shin Buddhism] said:

> I am the most evil person. There is no other skillful means [for my liberation]. I simply recite the name of Amida. I can attain birth in the land of the Greatest Bliss.[9]

Here the Greatest Bliss is a synonym for perfect freedom. Attaining birth in that land means attaining a life of perfect freedom.

"There is no other skillful means [for my liberation]" corresponds to "In going to Hell, I am alone."

"I simply recite the name of Amida" corresponds to the sudden transformation: "In going to the Pure Land, I am alone." Amida's calling voice is the only reality here. You are simply listening to Amida's calling voice. [And Amida's calling voice resonates in you and becomes your recitation of the name of Amida.] This means that you are in the Pure Land.

"Attaining birth in the land of the Greatest Bliss" is, therefore, an experience of perfect freedom within the sphere of self-awakening. Each person's individual self-awakening is a matter of being alone.

The four sentences in the *Records* correspond to these four sentences of Genshin. "The most evil person," needless to say, corresponds to "I am the only evil person," because "the most evil person" and "the only evil person" connote the same thing.

7

The word "the most" in "the most evil person" means that the person has all kinds of evil. It means that the world of evil is a stage on which the only actor is the self. It means that the world of evil exists only as a subjective reality within the context of self-awakening. The limitlessness of evil in its width and depth is described by the words "the most." And it is only within the sphere of self-awakening that we can see this limitless and endless evil. The singleness or oneness implied in the expression "I am alone" can contain limitlessness. The deepening that can be felt in the expression "the most evil" is the deepening of self-awakening. Self-awakening concerns the self alone, and "the most evil" refers to awakening to one's evilness, nothing else. Hence "the most evil person" is the person who has awakened to the fact that he is the only evil person in this world.

Further, the words "no other" in "There is no other skillful means [for my liberation]" mean that there are no other people, that one is all alone. "No other skillful means" means that nothing can connect one to other people, that one is totally abandoned. In this we can see the reality of the person who is falling into Hell all by himself.

The sentence: "I simply recite the name of Amida" is about recognition of oneness. At the very moment that a person falls into Hell all by himself, he is already made aware of absolute oneness. Since he, as oneness, meets with Amida, who is oneness, he simply recites the name of Amida, of oneness. The calling voice of Amida's oneness is reaching him and he is just responding to it with the voice of oneness. The self, which is one-sidedly determined to be in Hell, encounters Amida, who is one-sidedly determined to liberate the self. These two one-sidednesses are one and the same. That oneness and this oneness are identical. There cannot be two onenesses! One-sidedly determined Hell and one-sidedly determined birth in the land of Greatest Bliss are one and the same. Here we see the perfect freedom referred to in "I can attain birth in the land of Greatest Bliss."

In the final analysis, "I am the devil" is an expression of perfect freedom. Truth is making the self the devil. So our freedom is precisely the freedom to be evil.

Besides the freedom to be evil, no other freedom whatsoever is given to us. Hence, "You should not fear even evil."[10] We just receive the freedom to be evil, considering it our freedom—this is the real content of human freedom. Perfect freedom does not mean that we do something good. We are simply permitted to do as much evil as we want. This permission is mentioned in the passage [in the *Tannishō*] "because there is no evil that can hinder the Innermost Aspiration [or Vow] of Amida."[11]

"The freedom to be evil" into which we are liberated without any reservation, concern, fear, or anxiety—this is the real content of human freedom. As a matter of fact, freedom cannot take any other form. When scholars of ethics listen to statements like this, they will be quite astounded. But to our sorrow—(or to our joy)—one freedom, the freedom to be evil, is given to human beings. It means living the truth of impermanence itself—committing our total existence to the truth.

8

When a person who declares he is a devil is liberated and free, his freedom must be precisely the freedom of a devil. He can perform all kinds of evil acts. This is liberation into freedom.

Rev. Akegarasu listened to a voice coming from the heavens that said, "You should not fear even evil, because there is no evil that can hinder the Innermost Aspiration of Amida." So he could calmly say, "I am the devil." If he had not listened to the voice, he could not have uttered those words.

"You should not fear even evil" liberates us into the freedom to be evil. It is the only freedom for human beings and it is totally permitted to them; this indicates its absoluteness. Shinran's words at the end of Chapter 1 of the *Tannishō*, "You should not fear even evil," are his confession that "I am the devil." His words "there is no evil that can hinder the Innermost Aspiration of Amida" are his declaration of absolute freedom in the process of self-awakening. Rev. Akegarasu's sentence is a rephrasing of Shinran's words. Rev. Akegarasu goes through Shinran to Śākyamuni, to Śākyamuni's exact thought at the moment of his awakening.

In the expression "even evil" I detect the nuance that evil is the only thing there. Here is a shout of despair that Shinran cannot do anything but evil. When he is one-sidedly determined to be evil in this way, he experiences the "determinedness" in determined birth in the Pure Land. He recognizes the absolute oneness of Amida. Amida is allowing him to be what he is. Being what he is means being evil. Here human freedom is explained absolutely as the freedom to be evil, as nothing else. Thus we can boil our discussion down to this: Liberation is the freedom to be evil, nothing else. Those who do not recognize the freedom to be evil will never be able to understand religious freedom. They will never be able to know what true liberation is.

In the *Dharma Talks of Yogawa*, Genshin Sōzu says,

> Deluded ideas are the basic nature of a [foolish] ordinary person [like me]. Aside from deluded ideas, there is nothing that can be called the mind.[12]

Thus there is no freedom for human beings other than the freedom to have deluded ideas. Deluded ideas are allowed to be there. They are made to exist by truth. This freedom to have deluded ideas is the freedom to be evil. That deluded ideas are made to exist by truth means that there is only the freedom to be evil.

Charming indeed is the human being who takes delight in indulging in the freedom to be evil! Charming indeed is the human being who declares "I am free," revelling in the freedom to have deluded ideas!

Deluded ideas are the truth in human beings. They encompass all falsehoods, errors, and mistakes. It is precisely in deluded ideas that we discover truth, the subjective truth which exists in self-awakening. The fact that this world is false is simultaneously the truth that only the Buddha is true.[13]

9

A mass of errors, mistakes, and falsehoods—such are the deluded ideas that are the basic nature of a human being, that are the human being. When Genshin flatly declares, "Aside from deluded ideas, there is nothing that can be called the mind," I feel a free and freeing sensation. Here I see an unfettered, emancipated Genshin, who has the freedom to have deluded ideas and has calmly settled into it. He confesses, "I constantly create one illusion after another because of my deluded ideas." There is a liberating feeling, a feeling of truth in his absolute, decisive insight, "Aside from deluded ideas, there is nothing which can be called the mind."

I experience the same kind of liberating feeling when I read Prince Shōtoku's absolute insight, "This world is false." This insight, just as it is, crystallizes into, "Only the Buddha is true."

The postscript of the *Tannishō* says,

> Shinran said, "For a [foolish] ordinary person, loaded with desire and suffering, all things in this ever-changing world—this burning house—are empty, nonsensical, and false. Only the *nembutsu* is true."[14]

The words "only the *nembutsu*" describe a sudden reversal into absolute freedom—through an absolute, decisive insight. The *nembutsu* [*Namu-Amida-Butsu* (one who is awakened to the infinite because of bowing)][15] is itself the crucial phrase that marks the reversal in the statement "Absolute negation is simultaneously absolute affirmation."

Absolute reversal means that a thing is what it is; that a thing has no choice but to be what it is. It means that you should be what you are, that you have no choice but to be what you are. That you are what you are is freedom. To live life as it is, to live as you wish, to live as fully as possible, without reserve—this is freedom. It is no longer important to ask whether it is good or evil. The freedom to be what we are—nothing but this can be called freedom.

Our whole life, just as it is, our life in which "all things ... are empty, nonsensical, and false," is said to be "true." Our whole life, just as it is, is described by Shinran as "only the *nembutsu* is true."

Now it has become clear where freedom lies. The sentence "I am the devil" shows it to us.

The above analysis has gradually clarified the basic reason why Rev. Akegarasu called himself a devil. It is because he was a [foolish] ordinary person with deluded ideas. "Deluded ideas" means a restless and unconcentrated mind in which there is no logic or order.

Human existence, human life, is produced by causes and conditions. These causes and conditions are limitless and unfathomable. They cannot be grasped by the finite wisdom or intellect of human beings. Although human beings think that they control and regulate everything that surrounds their all-important selves, their lives are actually shaped by reciprocal relationships among the unfathomable causes and conditions in this infinite world. Their lives are a continual flow of so-called karma. Hence Shinran confessed, "Under certain karmic conditions, I might do anything."[16] This statement tersely says that a human being is "a being with deluded ideas."

10

Any action that is caused by deluded ideas is an evil action. It lacks consistency, system, order, and logic. It may be called a haphazard action. And can any of us claim that we are not living haphazardly? "Haphazard" may sound a little too unsophisticated. If I were to use a solemn philosophical term, it would be "actional intuition." Or I might just say "whimsical." Mephistopheles, in Goethe's *Faust*, defines human existence as whimsical existence. Human beings are whimsical, because the truth that makes them exist is none other than the truth of impermanence.

The limitless and unfathomable causes and conditions that I mentioned earlier are concrete aspects of the truth of impermanence. "Deluded ideas" are the form that the truth of impermanence takes in the subjective human self.

Some people, however, think that they can regulate their lives or actions in a rational and logical manner. I consider this view the worst of all deluded ideas, because it shows ignorance of the truth of impermanence.

As Bergson showed by his term *élan vital*, our thoughts simply chase after the traces left by the vital force of life. Bergson's term aptly expresses impermanence. Our thoughts simply trail after life; they cannot possibly regulate it. I call the above view the worst of all deluded ideas because it ignores this fact.

When we become aware that our own actions are purely illogical, haphazard, and whimsical, we utter a sigh of resignation—"Ahhh." This sigh says, "I am the devil." We thoroughly realize, "Oh, I am only a devil. I am not at all decent." We discover that our continuously changing self is full of deluded ideas. Our indecent, unregulated, irresponsible, self-indulgent, licentious, impure, orderless, whimsical actions—these we recognize as the actions of a devil. In the last analysis, we cannot possibly grasp the movement of the truth of impermanence. We are not God. If men, like God, knew everything about the movement of the truth of impermanence, nobody would make a mistake on the stock market!

Our irresponsible and haphazard actions, which come out of our ignorance, are millions of miles removed from so-called "good actions"—actions expected of us by ethics. Thus they must be regarded as evil actions. It is because of the truth of impermanence that human actions can only be evil actions. It is the truth of impermanence that does not allow human beings to commit anything but evil actions. This truth fills human beings with desire, suffering, and delusion. Therefore, "I am the devil" are words of truth. They express a subjective grasp of the truth of impermanence.

11

When the subjective self, which is filled with desire, suffering, and deluded ideas, recognizes that it cannot carry out anything but evil actions, it discovers its own true nature. It is a devil. This human truth, this grasp of the truth of impermanence as it is understood within the subjective human self, was Śākyamuni's exact thought at the moment of his awakening.

This was his awakening to the truth. The word "awaken" expresses a subjective grasp of truth better than the word "know." So we can say that Śākyamuni was awakened to the truth of impermanence. "I am the devil" is a subjective and concrete expression; his subjective grasp of the truth of impermanence is well expressed there. There is a sharp flash of truth in this statement. It is the crucial essence of Shinshū.

There is no way to know Buddhism except to encounter this one sentence. Indeed, there is nothing complicated here. There is only one flash, a flash of introspection.

People may talk a great deal about other things—about a general outline of Buddhism or a system of Buddhist thought, for example. But those things are all nonsense. They are only the useless undertakings of idle people, the sleep-talking of people with nothing better to do.

In Buddhism, one sentence is enough. One sharp flash of truth is enough. For Buddhism is a matter not of objective logic but of one flash of introspection. Are you a devil? If you say yes, your grasp of Buddhism is good enough.

Things like systems of doctrine are only scholars' sleep-talking. If you conceive, even slightly, of thought systems like the doctrines of

Kegon or the doctrines of Shin Buddhism, you are out of focus and millions of miles removed from religion. But this is what scholars do.

After you have discovered that you are a devil, what kind of thought system is that devil going to construct? If you say that you are going to construct a devil's doctrinal system, people will not be able to resist laughing at you. The fools who do this seriously are scholars of religion. They have nothing to do with *Shinshū*, which is summed up in the two words *shin* (true) and *shū* (religion). *Shinshū* is the realization that one is a devil, in the liquidation of the "good" self. It is being deprived of everything we have. This is the "nothingness" taught in Zen. There is no room for academicism. But in spite of this, scholars go on talking about such things as Shin Buddhist doctrine. Thus I cannot help calling scholars fools.

As long as there is dogma, there is no *Shinshū* (true religion). There is no room for even one fixed mode, thought, system, or idea in the world of religion. Even nothingness, if it is considered the doctrine of nothingness, is not in the sphere of true religion. The crucial essence of Shinshū is one sharp flash of truth. Matters of religion are decided in a moment. Because truth is impermanence, we are not able to advocate ideas as if they were fixed. The tremendous spiritual landscape of the person who really knows that he is a devil is expressed in the word *yū* (perfect peace).[17]

12

Thus *yū* (perfect peace) is grasped subjectively. It is the tremendous spiritual world of a person who does not have anything in himself. Rev. Akegarasu's one crucial sentence shows a straight path leading to it. I cannot help saying, "This sentence describes the crucial essence of Shinshū, or the deep meaning of the *nembutsu*." And "the reader can understand it easily," because it is just one sentence.

His one sentence is not a systematic exposition of the Dharma based on objective logic. Any attempt to relate one teaching to another by means of objective logic can do nothing at all to bring about a fundamental transformation of the subjective self. This fundamental transformation means a hundred-eighty degree turn. It means that a person who has not yet experienced liberation comes to experience it. For this transformation to occur, there must be a transition from objective logic to the point of view of the subjective self. A person who so far has only been concerned with the world in front of him must start to look into his inner world. This introspection takes place in a split second. He immediately sees what he really is. It is one sharp flash of introspection. It does not require any logical or doctrinal reasoning. If one reasons, "Since that is x, this is y; therefore the other is z," then only this logical relationship appears before one. One's self is unexamined.

Introspection tells one directly, "I am x." This is not a logical deduction like "Since that is x, this is y." It has to be intuited. "The reader can understand it easily," because it is a matter of intuition, of one sharp flash of introspection. In the world of religion, there is only introspection and intuition. There cannot be other things like logical deductions or doctrinal systems.

Such a term as "Buddhist thought" is the nonsensical creation of scholars. So far as the essence of Buddhism is concerned, there can be no thought or system of thought. Thus if a scholar starts to discuss Buddhist thought, we should realize that not a fragment of Buddhism can be found in his discussion.

There is only nothingness in Buddhism; there is no thought about nothingness. If the reader cannot understand it easily, it is not religion. The spiritual world of this nothingness is $y\bar{u}$.

$Y\bar{u}$ is Śākyamuni's nirvana. Nirvana literally means "extinction." Extinction of what, then? It is the extinction of reliance on one's own abilities. Reliance on one's own abilities is reduced to nothingness, and only a power beyond the self remains at work. The spiritual world of one who commits his total existence to that power is called $y\bar{u}$. The spiritual world of one who lives a totally free and unhindered life made possible by a power beyond the self—whose life is freedom itself—is called $y\bar{u}$.

A free life-style made possible by a power beyond the self is the actualization (*poiesis*)[18] of the concept of simplicity (*kanso*).[19] It is full of the creative activities of a fresh and vivid life. This is the content of nirvana, the real content of "extinction." In Śākyamuni's life it took the form of activities of great compassion. How can "I am the devil" become activities of great compassion? Because the self and the devil are merged into one.

13

If I am a devil, I am no different from any other evil person. I can instantly shake hands with any other evil person. We can embrace each other. This is the great compassionate heart of Śākyamuni. There is no room for distinguishing between good people and evil people. If we watch carefully, aren't so-called evil people good and so-called good people evil? Therefore, Shinran said, "I am totally ignorant as to what is good and what is evil."[20]

Such a tremendously rich, broad, and limitless spirit—a spirit that can embrace all things without excluding anything—is called *yū*. In the world of *yū* there is no narrow-minded discrimination between good and evil.

In this sense it should be said that Shinran's statement "I am totally ignorant as to what is good and what is evil" describes *yū*. It describes a total absence of narrow-mindedness, a total absence of roundabout and verbose reasoning.

Earlier I said that a life based on intuition entirely lacks any thought, any logical induction, deduction, or reasoning. That is natural because a life based on intuition is characterized by perfect peace (*yū*). Statements like Prince Shōtoku's "My foolish mind cannot understand it" describe the spirit and life of *yū*. If we say that our foolish minds cannot understand it, what logic, what thoughts, could we have?

"Tremendously broad and limitless"—without this expression, how could we describe the world in which an evil person is allowed to be what he is, allowed to live in freedom, and appreciates and enjoys the freedom to be evil? It is the very world of truth. If truth is what makes the existence of all things possible (all things, be they bad, good, beautiful, ugly, true, or false), *yū* is the world of that truth.

What enables us to reach this truth through introspection is the one crucial sentence, "I am the devil." Without introspection it is impossible to realize that the truth makes not only good but also evil exist.

Thus no matter how seriously one may, through objective logic, investigate what truth is and where it is, one will never be able to attain it and experience liberation through it. Scholars cannot grasp truth. Although they discuss truth as if they had a monopoly on it, they cannot in fact attain it or experience liberation. They merely play with words.

We cannot grasp truth itself by academicism or philosophy. Only introspection can enable us to do that. It is only in the world of thoroughgoing introspection, where one says, "I am totally ignorant as to what is good and what is evil," that for the first time one grasps and understands the truth that makes both good and evil exist. Scholars do not grasp this kind of truth because they always distinguish between good and evil. It is exactly because they distinguish that they are called scholars!

14

In this sense, "I am the devil" is the statement of truth. We can say that it manifests truth itself, and that it shows an immediate path to truth.

If freedom is realized only when one manifests truth, when one lives truth by becoming one with it, we can also say that this sentence manifests freedom, and that it shows an immediate path to freedom.

To intuit truth and manifest it is to become one with truth; it is to become truth and work as truth. Aside from this, there is no freedom. If this sentence is a perfect penetrating expression of truth, it reveals freedom, nothing else.

The one word that accurately describes this world of truth, this freedom, is yū. Buddhism can be summed up in this one word. Just as Zen masters once saw in the one word "nothingness" a perfect and succinct expression of Buddhism, so I now see in this word yū the all-contained totality of Buddhism. If one can penetrate this one word yū, one's understanding of Buddhism is complete.

I am talking about the importance of Rev. Akegarasu's sentence because it leads to yū. For example, how could we attain the above-mentioned nothingness without introspection? No matter how solemnly a person may repeat nothingness, if he does not have insight into his own evil—into the fact that he is an evil person, a devil, if his reliance on his own abilities is not smashed to pieces, how can he appreciate nothingness? If people think that they can realize a life of nothingness by eliminating their thoughts and ideas through Zen meditation, they will not be able to find the path to nothingness. Even if they were to spend eternity in the attempt, they would never be able to touch even slightly upon nothingness.

Rev. Akegarasu's one sentence describes this nothingness. Nothingness means the nothingness within introspection, the nullification of reliance on one's abilities. Such nothingness is absolute nothingness. And if the world of the self-determination of absolute nothingness develops here, then it is precisely the world of *yū*. The self-determination of absolute nothingness means the world of a power beyond the self. The world of a power beyond the self is the world of freedom. Such a rich world, where all things are made to exist as they are, is the world of *yū*.

In the sphere of *yū* all things, just as they are (be they good, evil, beautiful, ugly, true, or false) are made to exist. Not one thing is excluded. All things are embraced without exception. As long as there is discrimination, if A may be here but B may not, there is no Buddha-Dharma, no *yū*. The world of the Buddha-Dharma is most clearly revealed in the fact that it allows a devil to be what he is. People hate a devil more than anything else. Allowing such a being to exist clearly shows that the world of yū does not exclude anything.

15

The world of *yū* is a world in which all things are complete and perfect. There is a war in Vietnam. The People's Republic of China is experimenting with nuclear weapons. These incidents, just as they are, form a world in which all things are complete and perfect. This is a world in which all things are complete and perfect because both life and death exist. Who can say that such-and-such a life should not be? Who can say that such-and-such a death should not be? Both life and death already exist. Even if we were to declare that such-and-such a life should not happen, what could we do about the fact that it does? Even if we were to claim that such-and-such a death should not happen, what could we do when it does? Both life and death, just as they are, form a world in which all things are complete and perfect.

If this world had only one sort of life, or only one sort of death, it would not be interesting. Because it has various kinds of lives and deaths, it is rich, colorful, and gorgeous. It has good, evil, beauty, ugliness, truth, and falsehood. These things are endlessly changing into other things. What a great entertainer, spontaneous and ever fresh, this world is!

The term "nothing lacking" fits this world. Not only good but also evil are given to us. Since beauty by itself becomes monotonous, ugliness is given to us. How meticulously and elaborately truth has created this world! This world has both wealth and poverty, both joy and suffering, both diligence and laziness, both truth and falsehood. It seems to have been made in such a way that human beings will never get tired of living. It was made to be the world of life itself.

The world of life is a world of contradiction, a world of dialectic. If good does not coexist with evil, there is no dialectic, no contradiction, and therefore no life. If we desire life, we should not reject contradiction. Truth and life are directly connected. Thus life should be unequivocally defined as a function of truth.

The working of truth is life. Truth works dialectically as a contradiction; that is how life comes into existence. Life is neither good nor evil. It is neither beauty nor ugliness. It is neither truth nor falsehood. It is a single contradiction. It is truth itself. To appreciate and enjoy life means to appreciate and enjoy this type of life. One who appreciates and enjoys this type of life lives in the world of yū, where all things are complete and perfect.

When a person, at this present moment, can see the working of one absolute truth in every corner of this world and regard it as the working of eternal life, he can appreciate and enjoy eternal life. An appreciator and enjoyer of eternal life lives in the world of yū, where all things are complete and perfect.

My earlier definition of "life" may be enough for my purposes. However, as far as the working of truth is concerned, "eternal life" is a better and more comprehensive expression. Eternity has a touch or nuance of truth. We can fully recognize that all things in this world are complete and perfect when we intuit eternal life in the eternal now. Unless we come this far, our appreciation of *yū* is still not thorough.

16

What, then, is the relationship between eternal life and the self, which is a devil? It is the relationship between the infinite and the finite. Eternal life goes on, encompassing human lives and deaths. Eternal life is eternal life because it makes human beings live and die.

When finite beings (the many) encounter an infinite being (the one), the finite beings discover that they are devils. Finite beings are competitive. Since they compete with each other, they are relative beings. They cannot affirm their own existence without negating that of others. Finite beings' negation of other finite beings and their self-affirmation by means of this negation are "evil." The manner in which finite beings, relative beings, exist is "evil." They cannot possibly have the magnanimity of the absolute one, magnanimity which can embrace all beings.

Thus human beings are guilty of original sin; they are the many who rebel against the one, parts that reject the whole. Original sin is the basic manner in which human beings exist. Indeed, without rebelling against God, human beings cannot be human beings. Human beings are small universes that oppose the great universe, possessors of their own self-aware worlds, and self-aware cognizers of this world. They can be defined, basically, as beings who rebel against God.

It is therefore quite natural that there will be atheists (people who reject religion) as long as human beings are human beings. There is nothing surprising in this. The meaning of human existence is that a human being is a tiny part that rebels against the whole. Although the part is not the whole, it, as an independent being, claims to have some kind of wholeness. The claim to be whole is a claim to be a ruler. Hence attempts to negate others, to subdue them, and to force them to obey, are quite natural. The part's impersonation of the whole is called "evil." Such a self is called "a devil."

Eternal life—the real whole—makes such parts exist and entirely encompasses them. The infinite one splits itself into finite ones; this is how eternal life makes us exist as devils. If eternal life is entirely made up of groups of small devils, it is actually one great devil. God is the devil because he makes devils exist. The great devil which makes small devils exist is called God.

Do the so-called atheists not accept this kind of theism? As long as we acknowledge the existence of evil in this world, we cannot help but recognize God as the great devil.

The great devil does not oppose other beings. Thus he is called God, the nonopposing one, the absolute one. The great devil does not oppose small devils; he unconditionally embraces all of them. Thus he is called God rather than the devil.

17

The conversation between the Lord and Mephistopheles in the "Prologue in Heaven" of Goethe's *Faust* shows that the Lord is nothing but a great devil. We can assume that Goethe, at least, understood God in that way.

When finite ones discover themselves to be devils, the infinite one must be working behind the finite ones. And finite ones, becoming the one, must be seeing themselves as the many. The great devil must be teaching the small devils, "You are also devils." Since the many are contained in the one, since the many are the many because of the self-division of the one, the one works in the many and discovers itself as the many, as relative and finite ones. This process is described [by Dr. Nishida] as "the many are the one."

Since "the one is the many," "the many are the one."[21] This shows the process by which we awaken to the reality of the self. A devil is both a devil and an awakened one. In a devil who is made to exist by God, something divine works. It is the self-negation of the many. The many "return to," "take refuge in," or "entrust themselves to" the one that makes them exist. That is why "entrusting" is an expression of the deepest self-awakening.

Our liberation takes place only within that sphere of self-awakening in which we understand the relationship between the finite and the infinite. The principle, "The one is the many, and the many are the one," already speaks of liberation. The self-awakening indicated in it is precisely liberation.

The principle, "The one is the many, and the many are the one," is extremely important. If we can truly recognize this principle in the relationship between God and human beings, we have already experienced liberation. If a person often speaks about the principle but indulges in roundabout discussion like an unliberated person, he has not penetrated the real meaning of the principle.

The principle means this: God makes devils exist; and these devils return to God by self-negation, by self-awakening which shows them that they are devils.

Thus "the one is the many, and the many are the one" is the content of the spiritual world of *yū*. The many live out their own unique individualities. The world of *yū* is a beautiful and gorgeous picture scroll in which devils are competing with all their might. However, all those devils are made to exist entirely by God, by eternal life. They, just as they are, return to the one, the absolute one.

Each devil is liberated. He wholeheartedly lives his unique individual life, making use of all his resources. His life, just as it is, is unconditionally allowed and embraced by eternal life. This is the landscape of the world of *yū*. In this world there is no discrimination, no segregation, and no statements based on limited, one-sided human perspectives, like "This is good, but that is bad." A world in which all things are absolutely affirmed is the essence of *yū*.

18

Thus the sphere of *yū* is a world of thoroughgoing self-awakening, as discussed above. It is a world in which nothing has to be done because of human, ethical considerations. Because of absolute affirmation, both we and others are affirmed. We absolutely allow others to take any action that they wish to take of their own free will. Simultaneously we ourselves simply live and act as freely as we wish. This is the life of *yū*. The world of absolute affirmation—in which both the freedom of others and that of the self are simultaneously affirmed—is precisely the world of *yū*.

We must clearly understand where this absolute affirmation comes from. We must clarify the basis of absolute affirmation. It is absolute negation, self-negation. The sentence which fully shows this self-negation is Rev. Akegarasu's "I am the devil."

Absolute affirmation means that there is "no action of the self" (*mu-i*). It means that all things are affirmed by a power beyond the self. Any affirmation made by us as human beings, whether it concerns others or the self, is nothing but self-affirmation. When our self-affirmation is totally destroyed and we have "no action of the self," when we recognize that all things are made to exist and made to take place by eternal life, then we are liberated and have the freedom to do whatever we want to do. This is absolute affirmation.

This world, as it actually is, is just such a world of *yū*. It is the world of eternal life. I am made to live and die in it. Life is just made to be there, and death is just made to be there. I simply do what I want to do. That's all. I do it not because it has meaning. I do it not because I am told "thou shalt." Life just makes me take actions. This is my life. Thus I live and die freely.

Since I am already made to live in this actual world in which eternal life is manifested, what complaint could I have? What dissatisfaction or grudge could I have? I am simply living my life as fully as possible in each new situation. If death comes to me, I should accept it, because it is eternal life that makes death exist in me. Is there any person in this world who can refuse death? In their acceptance of death, all people recognize eternal life.

The fact that human beings die—this is proof of the existence of eternal life. Although many Western philosophers have attempted to prove the existence of God, was there even one philosopher who ever tried to do so by adducing the fact of human death? The same thing can be said about the existence of truth. The proof of the existence of truth is human death.

19

Nothing better reveals the truth than the fact that "man is mortal." It is truth that makes human beings die. So when human beings are about to die, they accept the truth. By accepting death, I mean recognizing it as it is, or thoroughly experiencing it as something beyond oneself. As long as human beings die, they will recognize the truth.

So far I have often used the term "truth." But it has now become clear in what situation human beings have to recognize the truth. Because of death, the final reality in human existence, all human beings have to admit the truth. Although they do not necessarily face imminent death, they all know that they are going to die. Thus we could say that all their lives, they recognize the truth. What, then, is truth? It is impermanence, eternal life. The life of one who recognizes this truth is called *yū*.

Therefore all people live in *yū* in some way or other. *Yū* is familiar to everybody. Thus we can find this one character *yū* in the dictionaries of the Chinese people, in their language. The realm in which everybody already lives is rediscovered in the light of subjective truth, in self-awakening, and is simply called *yū*. Since everybody without exception is made to exist by eternal life, the realm of truth must be common to all. In Rev. Akegarasu's one statement, we see the means by which we all can awaken to the source of our existence. This statement enables us to recognize, subjectively, the truth by which we are made to live and die.

The Easy Practice implied in the statement, "the reader can understand it easily" can be found in Rev. Akegarasu's statement. We have only to understand this one statement. It settles all problems. Dōgen said, "The most important thing in my life, my search for the way, had ended." These words can be said only when one understands this one statement. Why does Dōgen say, "The most important thing in my life, my search for the way, had ended"? Because he understood the truth. Because he had started to live a life of absolute freedom, having entered into the world of absolute affirmation. Because he had thoroughly entered into the realm of *yū*. All these experiences depend upon understanding this one statement.

This Easy Practice is the wonder of the Buddha-Dharma. Contrary to our expectation that we will attain absolute liberation only gradually, after performing difficult and painful practices, we can attain it instantly, at this very moment, by understanding that one statement. There is no room at all for such verbose, roundabout things as systems of Buddhist thought or systems of doctrine. The wonder of the Buddha-Dharma consists of one sharp flash of truth.

20

So far I have been exalting Rev. Akegarasu's one statement as the statement of truth. I have said that it describes the totality of Buddhism, just as it is, without anything missing. This is my Buddhism. It is precisely the Buddhism I received from Rev. Akegarasu. All I want to say about Buddhism is fully expressed in this statement. What need is there for me to say anything else? If someone visits me and asks, "What is Buddhism?," I don't know any other way of answering the question but to show him this statement. I answer, "This is Buddhism. I don't know anything else."

Shinran must have felt the same way about his teacher's writing, because he says in the epilogue that I quoted above, "It [Hōnen's Senjaku-shū] is indeed the rarest and most superior of texts. It is the highest and deepest treasure in all literature." Seeing such a superior text, such a literary treasure, in front of him, what need was there for Shinran to talk about any Buddhism beyond that text? Shinran is joyfully saying here, "Hōnen's one statement, nothing else, is my Buddhism." This joy made him write the Kyōgyōshinshō. That mind of Shinran that fully understood Buddhism in Hōnen's one statement could not help producing Shinran's main work.

Just as Shinran claims "I cannot go even a step beyond Hōnen. I see all of Buddhism in his teaching," I confess I cannot go even one step beyond this sentence of my teacher. Thus this one sentence is my only answer to the question, "What is Buddhism?" I have written this essay simply because I want to reveal "the highest and deepest" meaning contained in this sentence.

In saying "rarest and most superior," Shinran confessed that he did not have anything besides the one statement of Hōnen. "Rarest" means that it is the only thing for Shinran. "Most superior" means that there is nothing comparable to it. For Shinran, Hōnen's one statement was the highest and best. Thus, to the question "What is Buddhism?" Shinran would also answer, "It is Hōnen's one statement." In order to clarify this one statement, Shinran wrote his *Kyōgyōshinshō*.

I also cannot help but write; but I keep returning to my teacher's one sentence. My Buddhism starts with that sentence and ends with it. That sentence is alpha and omega. And, as far as I am concerned, that sentence is the religion of *yū*. I, in accordance with my personality, express it with the character *yū*. Thus I am discussing the content of *yū* when I discuss that sentence.

Here am I, who interpret Rev. Akegarasu's one sentence as the single character *yū*. Here am I, who describe Śākyamuni's one thought of genuine trust (or understanding) as *yū*. All things lie within the vast and limitless world of the Buddha-Dharma. But where can we encounter the Buddha-Dharma for the first time? I cannot help but answer that it is in this one sentence of Rev. Akegarasu.

How, then, does simplicity (*kanso*) come out of *yū*?

21

Śākyamuni, who was in the spiritual realm of *yū*, lived to the age of eighty. And Shinran lived to the age of ninety. Their lives were lives of *yū*. I understand this as the actualization (*poiesis*) of simplicity (*kanso*).

Yū exists when we commit all of our life and death to eternal life. In *yū* we do not have to force ourselves to live. There is nothing we have to do of our own accord. It is a realm where the self does not act. Furthermore, we do not have to force ourselves to die. It is a natural sphere of life where oughtness does not exist. When we commit ourselves to eternal life, when we know that eternal life will make us die when the time comes, death is not a problem, either.

Life and death are functions of eternal life, and as such they are beyond the self's control. They exist because they are made to exist by eternal life. So long as eternal life does not make us die, we live!

How does this life of *yū* appear in our daily life? It is the actualization of *kanso*. *Kanso* is an appearance of naturalness, of a power beyond the self, in which eternal life is totally controlling our lives. If we attempt to do something ourselves, relying on our own abilities, our life becomes non-*kanso*. If we totally give up reliance on our own abilities, our life and actions will be natural and spontaneous.

If we only have *yū*, that is good enough. We do not have to worry about *kanso*, which is the inevitable outcome of *yū*. *Kanso* is being what we are. Life as it is, life as it is made to exist by eternal life, life in which the self is forgotten—this is *kanso*. There is no set pattern for *kanso*; it is a patternless pattern. Patternless pattern is its most adequate definition. We may also call it self-forgetfulness or the self-determination of absolute nothingness.

For an example of *kanso*, consider an action of Tan-hsia T'ien-jen [a Zen monk in the T'ang dynasty]. He pulled a Buddha statue off the altar on which people were worshiping it, threw it into the yard, and urinated on it. The Zen master Nan-ch'uan's [748–835] cutting a cat in two is the same kind of action.[22] Such acts cannot be reasonably explained from a human point of view. Neither can human logic or reasoning comprehend Hōnen's statement "The meaning [of the *nembutsu*] is that it is beyond all human meaning."[23] We cannot tell what action is going to come out of a human being.

It is said that Norinaga Motoori [1730–1801, a famous Shintō scholar] sneaked into the room of his maid one night, and she slapped him in the face. The next morning she asked his students, "Is our master really a god? I slapped him in the face. What shall I do now?" This story is not so much a legend as a true description of Norinaga's life. This was his self-determination of absolute nothingness.

Indeed, unexpected things come out of human beings! Shinran aptly said, "Under certain karmic conditions, I might do anything." Since *kanso* is the life-style of a selfless person, we cannot tell what may come out of it. Whatever is conceived of in a human head is not called *kanso*.

22

In that sense *kanso* is a free life-style. A free life-style is the life-style of a selfless person. Thus something not expected even by oneself could happen. We should know that *kanso* never exists when things are planned out in a human head and carried out logically according to the plan. Such humanly conceived actions are not actions of *kanso*—actions that one does as eternal life makes one do them. Nor are they the actions of a free person.

The statement "The meaning [of the *nembutsu*] is that it is beyond all human meaning" must indicate that inconceivable actions will occur. If we do not understand *kanso* in exactly this way, the idea has no life. That which is conceived of and fits into a conceptual pattern in a human head, or which people agree to as reasonable, or which can be put into a system of thought—this sort of thing is not the fresh and lively thing called *kanso*. People talk about humanitarianism, or humanism, or rationalism. But *kanso* exists at the very point at which humanitarianism or rationalism has no effect at all. People may criticize this as irrational. But their criticism cannot bother a person of *kanso*. His life cannot be otherwise. Such is the landscape of *yū*, the spiritual landscape of the world which is beyond the self.

It is precisely irrationality that extinguishes the self. It smashes the roundabout reasoning, the logic, of human beings. In *kanso* there is a feeling of "I myself don't know why I did such a thing. I was overwhelmed and carried away by a power beyond me." *Kanso* does not include reasoning. It is not something that human logic can lead people to.

Kanso is simply the overflowing of life. It is *élan vital*. It is total liberation and freedom. It is "the meaning that is beyond all human meaning." Shinran recollected his teacher's words in the following way:

> He [Hōnen] said, "As far as the *nembutsu* is concerned, its meaning is that it is beyond all human meaning, because it is beyond my ability to fathom, explain, or conceive of it."[24]

Kanso comes out of *yū* just as the *nembutsu* comes out of genuine trust in Amida's Innermost Aspiration [or Vow]. The *nembutsu* does not come out because of our calculations or because it is logical. It comes out spontaneously and unexpectedly, because one suddenly discovers that one is being embraced by eternal life.

Kanso is the working of eternal life in human existence. It is not the work of human beings. The actions that emerge from the insight "I am the devil" cannot possibly be understood from an ordinary human perspective. The actions of a free person must always have qualities that people cannot understand, no matter how much they may think about them.

Such is the way that *kanso* comes out of *yū*. There is no room at all for making a conceptual pattern out of *kanso* or for claiming that such-and-such an action is *kanso*. The actions of a free person, which come out of the realization that "I am the devil," are called *kanso*.

23

With the one statement, "I am the devil," Rev. Akegarasu smashed to pieces everything like reason, intellect, wisdom, culture, scholarship, logic, and thought. He pointed out that the world of total self-transcendence can be realized only in that statement. The essence of freedom is there. It is absolute liberation.

Rev. Akegarasu was not a preacher who looked solemn or serious. He never said "O.K." to his small, limited self. Far from affirming his self, he kept on smashing his selves one after another, moment by moment. He never stayed in one place for even a second. His continual advances came out of that one sentence. He did not possess anything. Far from possessing things in this world, he was continually throwing away, one after the other, those selves that possessed something. He went, moment by moment, to the Tathāgata, who called to him, "Come empty-handed!"

In living such a life as his, one becomes the truth of impermanence itself. Rev. Akegarasu was an embodiment of impermanence—the truth that Śākyamuni taught. In other words, he was a Tathāgata. If Buddhahood can be realized in that one statement, that statement must have been the thought of Śākyamuni at the moment of his awakening. And I saw in my teacher the image of a perfectly free Tathāgata.

Rev. Akegarasu was precisely nothingness itself. He was the self-determination of absolute nothingness. Where else but in nothingness could people find Buddhism? There was nothing in my teacher that could be called "Buddhist thought." There was only nothingness, which transcends what is solemnly called "Buddhism."

In Rev. Akegarasu I simply saw a real human being. I saw a human being who was *kanso* itself. This human being came out of the spiritual realm of *yū*. He was simply in the sphere of *yū*.

Where can we meet such a human being? In that one sentence—nowhere else. I cannot help but praise it to the fullest. I need no other sentence in this world.

In my teacher, I encountered a real human being himself. My greatest happiness lies in this fact. And through him I was also able to see Śākyamuni face to face. It was my teacher who led me to Śākyamuni. Thus the Buddha-Dharma was fully revealed by Rev. Akegarasu. The Buddha-Dharma is that one sentence.

Thus the great compassion of Śākyamuni has come to me through Rev. Akegarasu; and it is reaching all people. I cannot possibly stop believing that all people will be liberated by this one sentence. I keep this one sentence and annihilate all of Buddhism. I regard all of historical Buddhism, the Buddhism that has developed throughout its long twenty-five-hundred-year history, as good-for-nothing nonsense.

I will declare: If you want to see the Buddha-Dharma, don't go around looking here and there! Look at this one sentence!

(3/6, 1965)

185

APPENDICES

Appendix 1

A Chronology of Haya Akegarasu

(Information about Manshi Kiyozawa, Akegarasu's teacher, and Shūichi Maida, Akegarasu's student, is italicized.)

1877 Born on July 12, in Kita-yasuda, Ishikawa Prefecture, as the only child of Enen Akegarasu, the seventeenth minister of the Myōtatsu-ji temple, a temple belonging to the Jōdo Shinshū Ōtani-ha (or Higashi Honganji) branch.

1882 (Age 5) Enters a grammar school.

1887 (10) Enen, Haya's father, dies at age forty-nine. Rev. Hōjō Fujitani, Enen's uncle, becomes Haya's guardian. Chiyono, Haya's mother, raises him, struggling with poverty.

1889 (12) Enters Kanazawa Jinjō Junior High School.

1891 (14) Ordained as a Buddhist minister.

1893 (16) In February, quits Kanazawa Jinjō Junior High School, mainly because of the school's excessive emphasis on English and westernization. In September, enters Kyoto Ōtani Jinjō Junior High School, being attracted to the school's emphasis on traditional Buddhist education. *Meets the Rev. Manshi Kiyozawa*, his English teacher, who is teaching Smiles' *Self-Help*. Becomes friends with Gesshō Sasaki.

1894 (17) *Rev. Kiyozawa undertakes ascetic practices and contracts a severe case of pulmonary tuberculosis. Thus after being Haya's English teacher for five months, Kiyozawa must recuperate in the town of Tarumi in Hyōgo Prefecture.* Haya deeply respects Kiyozawa. In final exam, Haya receives the second highest grade in the class.

1895 (18) In July, *Rev. Kiyozawa returns to Kyoto from Tarumi. He joins eleven other eminent Buddhists in submitting a reform proposal to Ōtani-ha headquarters.*

1896 (19) In July, graduates from Shinshū Daiichi Junior High School (i.e., the new name of Kyoto Ōtani Jinjō Junior High School). On August 19, receives *his first letter from Rev. Kiyozawa*. In September, enters Shinshū University. In October, the reformers, *headed by Rev. Kiyozawa*, start publishing a monthly journal called *Kyōkai Jigen* (Timely Words for the Religious World), a journal criticizing the policy of the Ōtani-ha headquarters. In November, participates in a student strike against the sect's headquarters and gets expelled from the university together with ninety-nine other students. Travels and explains the needs for reform.

1897 (20) In February, *Kiyozawa and several of his sympathizers are expelled from the Ōtani-ha sect. Kiyozawa loses his teaching position at Jinjō Junior High School.* Around this time, starts to edit *Mujin-tō* (Inexhaustible Light), a Buddhist journal. In April, readmitted to the university. In November, *Kiyozawa's reform group disbanded.*

1898 (21) In January, treated for venereal disease. Around this time, reads the *Tannishō* intensely, appreciating it as being designed for such a defiled being as he. In May, *Kiyozawa retires to his home temple in Ōhama and deepens his religious convictions. This is known as Kiyozawa's December Fan period.*

1899 (22) In October, the Ōtani-ha headquarters decides to transfer its recently reorganized university from Kyoto to Tokyo, rename it the Shinshū University, and *appoint Kiyozawa president.*

1900 (23) In July, graduates from Shinshū University. Receives scholarship to study at the Tokyo Foreign Language School, majoring in Russian. At this point, Haya believes that he is not qualified to become a Buddhist minister because of his immorality and should work for world peace as a secular person. *Kiyozawa is against Haya's becoming a diplomat.* In September, moves to Tokyo and enters the Tokyo Foreign Language School. *Lives at Kiyozawa's residence.* In November, *Kiyozawa's residence, where Kiyozawa and fourteen other individuals, including Haya, live, is officially named "Kōkō-dō dormitory."* Haya frequently participates in discussions *conducted by Kiyozawa.*

1901 (24) In January, the first issue of *Seishin-kai* (Spiritual World), *a journal headed by Kiyozawa*, published. Haya, its managing editor, writes its opening statement. In October, Tokyo Shinshū University (present

Ōtani University) opens *with Kiyozawa as its first president.* In November, *Kiyozawa and his students start a weekly lecture meeting every Sunday at Kōkō-dō.*

1902 (25) In Spring, reads the *Tannishō* seriously. In September, *Kiyozawa sends Haya to Dr. Hiroyuki Katō, former president of Tokyo University, in response to Dr. Katō's request for a more detailed explanation of Kiyozawa's article "Peace Beyond Ethics."* In December, marries Fusako Yamada, a younger sister of Gesshō Sasaki, his close friend. *This year is a turbulent year for Kiyozawa. On June 5 his oldest son dies of sarcoma, and on October 6 his wife dies of tuberculosis. On October 22 he resigns from the position of president of the Tokyo Shinshū University because of a student strike. In November Kiyozawa returns to his temple in Ōhama.*

1903 (26) In March, *visits Kiyozawa at Ōhama.* In April, *Kiyozawa's second son dies.* On May 30, *one week before his death, Kiyozawa writes his final work, "My Religious Conviction," and mails it to Haya.* On June 6, *Kiyozawa dies at age forty. Having been informed of Kiyozawa's critical condition by telegram, Haya and two other students of Kiyozawa immediately head for Kiyozawa's temple; but he dies before they arrive.*

1907 (30) In June and July, edits *the complete works of Kiyozawa.*

1908 (31) In May, suffers from tuberculosis which threatens his life.

1909 (32) In June, participates in *the seventh [i.e., special] memorial service for Kiyozawa.*

1910 (33) Haya's criticism of the traditionalists, his assertion that merely chanting holy scriptures is useless and faith should be experienced in one's personal life, angers some Shinshū followers. They appeal to the Ōtani-ha headquarters, claiming that Haya is a heretic. In June, headquarters warns Haya about his lectures and writings. In August, holds his first summer retreat at his temple.

1911 (34) His *Lectures on the Tannishō* published.

1912 (35) In July, the Meiji Emperor dies. Haya observes fifty days of mourning; reads the Pure Land Triple Sutra every morning and keeps to a vegetarian diet. In September, immediately after the end of the mourning period, Fusako, his wife, contracts tuberculosis. Stays home and takes care of his wife.

1913 (36) In February, Fusako dies at age twenty-seven. In June, the *Complete Works of Manshi Kiyozawa* published.

1914 (37) In July, marries Fusa, Rev. Kakushin Imagawa's oldest daughter.

1915 (38) (1/29) The *Chūgai Nippō*, a Buddhist newspaper, carries an article entitled "A Rumor about Mr. Akegarasu" which calls Haya "a sex maniac." (2/5) The *Chūgai Nippō* again publishes an article on the scandal about Haya. In April, resigns from the leadership of the Kōkō-dō group.

1916 (39) In April, the Rev. Ruikotsu Matani, the author of the newspaper article "A Rumor about Mr. Akegarasu," writes to Haya and expresses his respect for him. (8/30–10/10) A trip to Okinawa. In October, the Kōkō-dō dormitory ceases to exist.

1917 (40) In April, meets the Rev. Ruikotsu Matani personally for the first time.

1918 (41) In September, starts to study the *Daimuryōju-kyō* (or *Larger Sukhāvatīvyūha-sūtra*) seriously.

1919 (42) In January, meets Miss Toyoko Haratani, who later becomes Haya's devoted friend and student. During this year his eyesight gradually gets weaker.

1920 (43) His *Before and After Rebirth* published.

1921 (44) In January, opens a publishing house called Kōsō-sha (or Nioigusa-sha) and starts publication of a series of his books entitled *Koso-Sosho*. This series continues to 1925, totaling twelve books. In April, his *Declaration of an Independent Person* published. In November, his *The Advancing One* published.

1922 (45) In January, starts publishing *Yaku'ōju* (Tree of the Medicine King), his personal journal. In October, starts publishing the *Kitayasuda Pamphlets*.

1924 (47) In January, his mother, Chiyono, dies at age seventy-five. (6/1–3) Gives a three-day lecture series at Kanazawa city hall *which eighteen-year-old Shūichi Maida attends*. In December, Miss Toyoko Haratani, his close friend, dies of peritonitis at age twenty-nine.

1926 (49) In March, the Rev. Gesshō Sasaki, his close friend, dies at age fifty-two. (11/30) Starts a trip to India.

1927 (50) (2/12) Ends his trip to India and starts a trip to Europe from India. (2/12 to 7/15) A trip to Europe.

1929 (52) (4/5 to 8/12) A trip to the U.S.A.

1933 (56) (1/30 to 4/29) A trip to Hawaii. (9/28 to 11/8) A trip to Formosa. In this year loses his eyesight completely.

1935 (58) Starts publication of *Gan'e* (Wisdom of the Vow), his monthly personal journal.

1943 (66) *Accompanying Prof. Gyōshō Shimizu, president of Ishikawa Teachers' College for Women, Shūichi Maida visits Haya for the first time. This is nineteen years after Maida first listened to Haya. (8/15–21) Maida attends Haya's thirty-fourth summer retreat. From this year until the death of Haya, Maida attends all of his summer retreats.*

1944 (67) Discontinues *Gan'e* after May issue and starts a new monthly journal entitled *Dōki* (Same Refuge).

1945 (68) From January to July, bedridden with tuberculosis. During this period, believes that his death is near.

1946 (69) In January, *Maida visits Haya and tells him about his desire to leave his family and job and go to Nagano to engage in Buddhist activities. Haya strongly encourages him to do so.* In June and October, visits Nagano to give lectures. *Visits Maida there.*

1947 (70) In June visits Nagano. *Visits Maida there.* In September, has an eye operation.

1950 (73) Donates his 60,000 books to the University of Kanazawa. In June, makes a lecture tour in Nagano. *Visits Maida there.*

1951 (74) In February, becomes the head administrative officer of the Ōtani-ha headquarters. In November, makes a lecture tour in Nagano *in response to a request from Maida.* In December, discontinues *Dōki.*

1952 (75) (1/1) Starts publication of *Kōdaiye* (Great Assembly), his monthly personal journal, *with Shūichi Maida as managing editor.* (7/5) *Shishiku* (Lion's Roar), a collection of excerpts from Haya's writings, *edited by Maida,* published.

1953 (76) (1/12) Submits letter of resignation as head executive officer of
Ōtani-ha headquarters. (5/16–18) Visits Nagano to give a commemorative lecture upon the founding of Kaiun-dō, *Maida's learning center.*
(7/12) His students celebrate his seventy-seventh birthday and decide
to build for him the *Rōsendō* (December Fan Hall). (10/12–12/31)
Hospitalized with intestinal catarrh.

1954 (77) (1/5) His *Kubon Ōjōnin* (Nine Types of People Who Are Born in
the Pure Land), *edited by Maida,* published. (2/23–25) *Maida visits
Haya in a hospital.* (5/20) His *Zettai Tariki no Daidō* (The Great Path
of the Absolute Power Beyond the Self), *edited by Maida,* published.
(8/19–21) Holds his forty-fifth summer retreat at his temple. (8/20)
Holds commemorative service for the inauguration of the December
Fan Hall at his temple. (8/27) Dies. (8/30) His *Yo-to-tomoni Yo-wo koen*
(Transcend This World Together with This World!), *edited by Maida,*
published. (9/1) The final issue of *Kōdaiye* published. (10/1) The first
issue of *Kōsō* (Orchid), *edited by Maida,* published. (12/) *Maida resigns
from editorship of Kōsō.*

Appendix 2

The *Tannishō*, Chapter 2

*(Statements quoted in Maida's essays, "The Words of the Good Person,"
"Even If I Were To Be Deceived" and others, are italicized.)*

Shinran said:

You have all travelled through more than ten provinces at the risk of your
lives solely in order to see me and to ask me how to be born in the land of
Utmost Bliss. But if you imagine that I know of ways to attain birth other
than the *nembutsu*, or if you imagine that I know the Buddhist scriptures,
you are greatly mistaken. If that is what you are looking for, you should
visit the many extremely distinguished scholars in Nara and on Mt. Hiei,
and hear their detailed explanations of what is essential for birth in the Pure
Land.

The good person [my teacher Hōnen] said, "Just say the nembutsu *and be
liberated by Amida." As far as I, Shinran, am concerned, I just accept and
trust his words. That's all.*

I am totally ignorant as to whether the nembutsu *is truly the cause of
my attaining birth in the Pure Land or whether it is a karmic action because
of which I must fall into Hell. Even if I were to be deceived by Hōnen
Shōnin, even if I were to fall into Hell because of saying the* nembutsu,
I would not regret it. If it were possible for me to become a Buddha
by performing some other practice, but I fell into Hell because of saying the *nembutsu*, I might well regret that I had been deceived by him. *But
since I am incapable of any religious practice whatsoever, Hell is my only
home.*

If Amida's Innermost Aspiration [or Vow] is true, Śākyamuni's teachings
cannot be false. If the Buddha's teachings are true, Shan-tao's commentaries
cannot be false. If Shan-tao's commentaries are true, how can the words of
Hōnen be deceptive? And if Hōnen's words are true, then what I, Shinran, say
surely cannot be meaningless.

Such is the understanding of the foolish person that I am. Beyond this, whether you take up the nembutsu *and entrust yourself to it, or reject it, is entirely your own decision.*

(*Taishō Shinshū Daizōkyō*, vol. 83, p. 728, b 8–c 15)

Appendix 3

The Source of Akegarasu's Statement, "The flame from the cremation of my entire self is my only liberation"

(The statement quoted in Maida's essay "Symphony of the Flame" is italicized.)

Radiance of the flame that burns my self! This flame that my karmic evil has created is covering the earth, flaring up, and scorching heaven. Nowhere can I find a place for my feet, for my body. Nowhere can I find a refuge for my soul. All the people and things that I have relied on are swallowed up by the karmic flame. They are being fiercely consumed. Even the gods and Buddhas in the heavens whom I once revered are burning in the karmic flame.

For a long time I have tried hard to extinguish this karmic flame. Having found that it is impossible to do so, I have attempted, at least, to run away from it. Thus I have sought refuge in people and things. Eventually I prayed to gods and Buddhas. I sought power in the *nembutsu*. But all these efforts were in vain. The terrible karmic flame is assailing me moment after moment. I scream, "I don't want to burn, I don't want to die." But now I crouch in silence and writhe in despair. Nothing can stop the fire. The raging fire advances to my legs, arms, and head. Before I know it, I am standing in the middle of the fire like *Acala*, the god of fire. Now the fire covers my whole body. It has reached my soul.

"Oh, total combustion! My life is finished!" With this shout, I hurl myself into the fire. How strange! At this moment I gain a new life. Spirit of Burning, radiant with the karmic flame! Spirit of Peace, illuminating the entire universe!

Permeated by the karmic flame that is consuming the entire universe, my spirit is advancing dynamically, without regret and fear, without doubt or hesitation.

If a person had not been frightened, and then grieved, cried, and mourned because of the flame that was burning up his body and mind, how could he gain a new life? Only a person who is permeated by and becomes one with the destructive karmic fire can embody radiance. *The flame from the crema-tion of my entire self is my only liberation.*

(Akegarasu, Haya. *Declaration of an Independent Person* in *Akegarasu Haya Zenshū* [Complete Works of Haya Akegarasu]. Part Two, Vol. 2. Ishikawa, Japan: Myōtatsu-ji, 1956–60, pp. 266–67.)

Appendix 4

The Source of Akegarasu's Statement, "I am the devil"

(The statement quoted in Maida's essay "The Crucial Essence of Shinshū" is italicized.)

Thus Siddhārtha realized that none of the traditional Indian religious theories could liberate him. He thought that he could be liberated through ascetic practices. He climbed the Gayāśīrṣa Hill on the east side of the Nairañjanā River and started to engage in ascetic practices according to Brahmanic teachings. Up to this time, Siddhārtha's father had provided food for him; and he was accompanied by five fellow mendicants such as Kauṇḍinya, his former retainers. But now he refused to accept his father's support. He ordered the five mendicants to leave, but they refused to do so.

For the next six years he ate one bowl of sesame or one bowl of rice a day. Or he ate only one bowl of sesame and one bowl of rice every two to seven days. If he happened to see a beggar, he gave him whatever food he had. The five mendicants also engaged in ascetic practices.

Although Siddhārtha engaged in these intense ascetic practices, he did not experience anything except bodily exhaustion. Far from attaining awakening, he realized that desires and deluded ideas were persistently appearing one after another in his mind. He was so emaciated that his breath seemed to have already stopped. Some people thought he had already died.

Then he came to the conclusion that neither the doctrines nor the practices of traditional Indian religions could liberate him. There arose in his mind a great doubt, a doubt that Jesus shouted on the cross, "My God, my God, why hast thou forsaken me?" Siddhārtha felt that his mind was increasingly overshadowed by darkness. Thus although the five mendicants objected, Siddhārtha left the mountain, resolutely abandoning the old religions, the old gods. He left the mountain more depressed than he was when he climbed it.

The five mendicants gave up on him, saying, "You are a failure." "Failure"! What a dear word it is! If Siddhārtha had not been a failure by the

199

standards of traditional Indian religions, he would not have created a new religion of self-awakening. His free spirit radiated in the darkness. He bathed his tired, totally emaciated body in the Nairañjanā River, but he could not climb up on the bank of the river without holding on to grass.

Just as he washed the filth from his body in the Nairañjanā River, he likewise deserted the ascetic disciplinary practices of the old religions. He needed this spiritual cleansing before he entered the new path of self-awakening. Only a person who has failed at an old religion can truly create a new spiritual world ...

At dawn, Siddhārtha took a bowl and went to a huge Bodhi Tree in order to beg for food. There he met a maiden named Sujātā, a daughter of Senāpati, a rich man in Uruvilvā. She came to offer fresh milk to the tree because her prayer for love had been granted. Having seen the dignified Siddhārtha from behind, she believed that he was the spirit of the tree and offered him refined milk on a golden tray. Since he had stopped the ascetic practices that forbade him to accept offerings from a woman, he now received it freely, without hesitation. He gradually regained his physical strength. Then he placed grass, which was offered by a shepherd, under the Bodhi Tree and sat on it to meditate. It is said that he continued this meditation for forty-nine days. This was to be his final practice before awakening. With a firm determination that he would not move from the seat until he experienced awakening, he quietly entered into meditation.

Now Siddhārtha had nothing in his being, no family, no religion, no teacher, and no disciple. He was all alone. He had only innermost aspiration— a desire to seek the way. As he sat quietly all by himself, he noticed that against his will, one deluded idea after another was arising in his mind.

His biographers have personified his deluded ideas and described them as the work of the devil. Unless we get rid of all restraints and seek the path all by ourselves, we cannot see the devil clearly.

The king of devils contrived all kinds of intimidation and seduction in order to distract Siddhārtha from the path of truth-seeking. He used such weapons as swords and spears. He used the coquettish charm of beautiful women. When the attack of the devils' army reached its peak, all of Siddhārtha's guardian gods, such as Nāgarāja, Brahmā, and Indra, were terrified and fled to their own countries ...

This was the most important event in Siddhārtha's life. The timid Nāgarāja reminds me of Peter, who was sleeping on the night when Jesus was arrested. When we have easy and comfortable lives, we believe in the protection of the gods. It is an extremely low type of religious view to say, "I have a very happy life thanks to the protection of the gods and Buddhas. This year has been a good year thanks to the protection of the Shintō deities." Such gods and Buddhas will immediately disappear when a devils' army violently assails our minds. They will leave us alone before the devils' army.

Siddhārtha now became a person "on the cross." He had nothing to rely on in his mind. He was absolutely alone. He was facing the devil in darkness, in the total absence of gods or Buddhas. Without any resistance, he was staring at the devil, who was appearing as a devils' army and as beautiful women.

The final phase in Siddhārtha's self-examination was his encounter with the devil. So far Siddhārtha had thought that he had something good in his mind. But now, at this ultimate point, he could see nothing in his mind but the devil. Without evading or fearing the devil, he calmly watched him. When the morning star shone at dawn on the eighth day of December, Siddhārtha, who was thirty-five, suddenly attained his great awakening. The content of his great awakening was "In the heavens and on the earth, my aloneness is noble." This means that in the heavens and on the earth, there is no person and no god to rely on—that my aloneness is noble.

The traditional account of how Siddhārtha attained awakening is as follows:

It was a little before sunset that Siddhārtha, the Bodhisattva, won a glorious victory over his arrogant enemies. Then he entered into very deep meditation. The ends of the branches of the Bodhi Tree bent down as if they were embracing the Bodhisattva's robe.

On the first night, the Bodhisattva, with utmost concentration of mind, thought and examined the law of causation that underlies all existing things. He thought: Pain and suffering certainly exist in this world; pain and suffering exist because of birth from a mother's womb; birth exists because of becoming, a moral condition produced by good or evil actions or by their influence; becoming exists because of attachment; attachment exists because of craving; craving exists because of perception; perception exists because of contact; contact exists because of the six sense organs; the six sense organs exist because of names and forms, i.e., objectifications of things by the mind; names and forms exist because of false knowledge; false knowledge exists because of imagination; imagination exists because of ignorance.

Having investigated the law of causation that consists of these twelve links and come to ignorance, the fundamental cause, the Bodhisattva said to himself:

Ignorance is the first cause of all the phenomena that I am now creating in my mind. It is from ignorance that both the world and the beings in it are produced. This ignorance is the cause of that universal delusion that afflicts all humans and other sentient beings. How, then, can ignorance be eliminated? Undoubtedly, it can be eliminated by wisdom, by true knowledge. When I am illumined by the light given by wisdom, I can clearly understand the emptiness of all things. I am now freed from the delusion that makes one believe the nonexistent to be existent. The power that makes me imagine the nonexistent to be existent is gone now. Hence, the false knowledge, which causes names and forms, six sense organs, contact, perception, craving, attachment, becoming, birth, and suffering of old age and death, is gone now.

Then the Bodhisattva further declared:

The wisdom of the four noble truths destroys the darkness of ignorance. It liberates me from the whirlpool of becoming. It is the true light that generates the true knowledge that frees me from delusion. The four noble truths are: (1) that suffering is inherent in human existence; (2) that insatiable desire for self-satisfaction is the cause of suffering; (3) that it is possible to destroy desire, i.e., to realize my liberation; and (4) that only those who practice the eightfold path—right view, right thought, right speech, right action, right effort, right occupation, right mindfulness, and right concentration—can eliminate desire.

At this point, the Bodhisattva acquired a firm and immovable mind, a perfectly concentrated mind, a mind liberated from all desires, a mind always warm and gentle, and a mind filled with deep compassion for all sentient beings.

After Siddhārtha carefully watched the devil, he experienced awakening when he said, "Oh, ignorance!" Awakening itself is light, but its content is ignorance. When he said, "Oh, ignorance," his ignorance had already disappeared. But this disappearance was not a disappearance in the usual sense. If he had shouted, "Oh, light!," ignorance would have immediately appeared.

For a long time, I wanted to know Śākyamuni's exact thought at the moment of his awakening. But I could not understand it. Initially I thought that Śākyamuni awakened to his Buddha-nature. This was probably so, but I could hardly understand that within the context of my own life.

This year I have come to understand that Śākyamuni's exact thought at the moment of his awakening was expressed in his shout "Oh, ignorance!" "Oh, ignorance!" means "Oh, darkness!" When Śākyamuni said this, the devil whom he saw face to face was not actually a devil in front of him, but was his own real self. Thus his conquering the devil meant his becoming the devil. *In this sense, Śākyamuni's exact thought at the moment of his awakening was his realization that "I am the devil."* When he had this great awakening, a tremendous sphere of oneness—in which he became completely one with all things—opened up for him. The *Avatamsaka-sūtra* depicts the brilliance of this great awakening that "I am the devil." Because Śākyamuni came to have such an awakening, he was called a Buddha, an Awakened One. Therefore, the Buddha was the devil. The devil was the Buddha. Ordinary people may not understand what I am saying here. Probably no one has ever described Śākyamuni's experience in this way. But if we do not understand the realization that "I am the devil," or the shout, "Oh, ignorance!," or the great awakening, we will never understand such teachings as "samsara is simultaneously nirvana" or "evil passions (*kleśa*) are simultaneously awakening (*bodhi*)." When we have this realization, we can truly understand the statement, "In the heavens and on the earth my aloneness is noble."

When the good gods have all left one's mind and only the devil fills it, the subjective self is filled with the devil. This is a world in which the subject and the object are one, in which the Buddha and the devil are one. Unless we come this far, we cannot understand the meaning of Amida's Vow—that Amida's self-identification with the lowest types of beings, with darkness itself, is the heart of his Vow to liberate all beings.

Here it appears to me that the Buddha under the Bodhi Tree and Jesus on the cross shared the same spiritual awareness. Further, I assume that Shinran had the same awareness when he said, "Since I am incapable of any religious practice whatsoever, Hell is my only home."

(Akegarasu, Haya. *Before and After Rebirth* in *Akegarasu Haya Zenshū*. Part Two, Vol. 2. pp. 188–93.)

Notes

Translator's Introduction

1. *Taishō Shinshū Daizōkyō* (hereafter abbreviated as T.), ed. by Junjirō Takakusu and Kaikyoku Watanabe, vol. 83 (Tokyo: Daizō Shuppan-sha, 1931), p. 728, a 19–20.

2. T. vol. 82, p. 3, c 1. See p. 33.

3. Cf. Manshi Kiyozawa, *December Fan: The Buddhist Essays of Manshi Kiyozawa*, trans. by Nobuo Haneda (Kyoto: Higashi Honganji, 1984).

4. Haya Akegarasu, *Akegarasu Haya Zenshū* (The Complete Works of Haya Akegarasu), part two, vol. 2 (Ishikawa, Japan: Myōtatsu-ji, 1956–60), p. 147.

5. For the traditional account of the meditation Śākyamuni experienced immediately before his attainment of Buddhahood, see Appendix 4.

6. T. vol. 2, p. 1, a 13.

7. The total death (or negation) of the self that Śākyamuni experienced is the core of Buddhism. To describe the subjective reality that Śākyamuni discovered, he and his followers used such terms as "nirvana (extinction)," "selflessness," "emptiness," and "nothingness."

Similarly, Pure Land masters like Hōnen and Shinran emphasized the importance of viewing the self as empty and insignificant. They described their basic nature with terms such as "evil," "ignorant," and "foolish."

In modern Japan, this negative view of the self was developed by individuals like Kiyozawa and Akegarasu. For example, Kiyozawa called himself "a fan in December," i.e., a good-for-nothing thing. Akegarasu interpreted Śākyamuni's awakening experience as follows:

> Śākyamuni's exact thought at the moment of his awakening was his realization that "I am the devil."

(See Appendix 4)

Maida considers this statement of Akegarasu a Copernican Revolution in Buddhism, because it clearly reconfirmed the core of Śākyamuni's awareness.

8. For a discussion of *shinjin*, see Shūichi Maida, *The Evil Person: Essays on Shin Buddhism*, trans. by Nobuo Haneda (Los Angeles: Higashi Honganji North American Translation Center, 1989), pp. 3–8.

9. T. vol. 83, p. 729, b 1–2. See p. 110 below.

10. Cf. *Dīgha-nikāya*, ed. by Nanavasa Thera (Colombo, 1929), vol. 2, pp. 61–2.

11. See chap. 10, n. 2 (pp. 209–210).

12. See p. 98 below.

13. T. vol. 2, p. 161, c 29. See p. 97 below.

14. The teacher for Kiyozawa was Shinran. Cf. Manshi Kiyozawa, *December Fan*, pp. 45–6.

15. Ibid., p. 728, b 19–28. Cf. Appendix 2 and p. 106.

1. Meeting with Impermanence

1. T. vol. 12, p. 267, a 21–b 18.

2. The Most Important Thing in My Life

1. T. vol. 82, p. 3, c 1.

2. Ibid., p. 15, b 9–10.

3. Ibid., p. 191, c 23–5.

4. Haya Akegarasu, *Akegarasu Haya Zenshū*, part one, vol. 1, pp. 225–89.

5. Cf. Shūichi Maida, *The Evil Person*, pp. 15–8.

3. Standing-Death

1. For the meaning of the *nembutsu*, see p. 11 above. Cf. Shūichi Maida, *The Evil Person*, p. 8.

2. T. vol. 37, p. 27, a 7.

4. Nothingness

1. Haya Akegarasu, *Akegarasu Haya Zenshū*, part three, vol. 5, p. 150.

5. Rev. Akegarasu and Rev. Kiyozawa

1. This quotation is slightly different from Akegarasu's original poem. For the original poem, see p. 45 above.

2. *Kiyozawa Manshi Zenshū* (The Complete Works of Manshi Kiyozawa), ed. by Haya Akegarasu and Kengyō Nishimura, vol. 7 (Kyoto: Hōzōkan, 1955), pp. 343–465. Cf. Manshi Kiyozawa, *December Fan*, pp. 25–9.

3. Ibid., p. 462. Cf. Manshi Kiyozawa, *December Fan*, p. 29.

4. *Bombu* (Skt. *pṛthag-jana*, "[foolish] ordinary person"). This is an important term in Shin Buddhism, one with which one is supposed to identify oneself.

5. Bankei, *Bankei Zenji Goroku* (The Record of the Words of the Zen Master Bankei), ed. by D. T. Suzuki (Tokyo: Iwanami shoten, 1941), p. 35.

6. *Zettai-mu no jiko-gentei* (the self-determination of absolute nothingness), Dr. Kitarō Nishida's term. Cf. Kitarō Nishida, *Nishida Kitarō Zenshū* (The Complete Works of Kitarō Nishida), vol. 6 (Tokyo: Iwanami shoten, 1965), pp. 19, 37; Keiji Nishitani, *Religion and Nothingness* (Berkeley and Los Angeles: University of California Press, 1982), pp. 246, 256–7.

7. The statement "Form is emptiness and emptiness is form" is found in the *Heart Sutra*, which is known as the *prajñā-pāramitā* logic of negation. By negating human attachment to both extremes, i.e., to existence (or form) and to nonexistence (or emptiness), it is designed to make one gain insight into reality as it is—as manifesting the flow of life or the truth of impermanence. This insight is also called the Middle Path because it understands things neither as existence nor as nonexistence.

8. *Heijōtei* (flat-ordinariness), a term coined by Dr. Kitarō Nishida. Cf. Kitarō Nishida, *Nishida Kitarō Zenshū*, vol. 9, p. 303.

9. The main writing of Shinran. T. vol. 83, pp. 589–643.

10. T. vol. 83, pp. 728–35. Cf. *Tannishō: A Primer*, trans. by Dennis Hirota (Kyoto: Ryūkoku University, 1982).

11. This article "Spiritual Awareness (*seishin-shugi*)" is found in *Seishin-kai* (Spiritual World) Journal, *Kiyozawa Manshi Zenshū*, vol. 6, pp. 2–5. For an English translation of this article, see *December Fan*, pp. 15–8.

12. Shūichi Maida, *Maida Shūichi Zenshū* (The Complete Works of Shūichi Maida), vol. 4, pp. 295–536 (Nagano, Japan: Maida Shūichi Zenshū Kankōkai, 1969–71).

13. Haya Akegarasu, *Akegarasu Haya Zenshū*, part two, vol. 10, pp. 393–5.

14. Cf. Appendix 4 (p. 201).

15. *Sumiyaka ni hombunnin nari* (Instantly be what you really are). T. vol. 82, p. 23, c 29.

16. Cf. Manshi Kiyozawa, *December Fan*, p. 90.

17. In 1921, Akegarasu opened his personal publishing house named Kōsō-sha (or Nioigusa-sha) and started the publication of a series of his books entitled the *Kōsō-Sōsho* series. This series contains twelve books published from 1921 to 1925. Cf. *Akegarasu Haya Zenshū*, part two, vols. 3–5.

18. Although Maida here mentions Dr. Enryō Inouye [1858–1919, a famous Buddhist philosopher], it was actually Dr. Hiroyuki Katō [1836–1916, a philosopher and educator who once was president of Tokyo Imperial University] that Akegarasu met.

19. *Heijō-buji* (Everything is ordinary and nothing is special). T. vol. 47, p. 498, a 16–7.

6. The December Fan Hall

1. T. vol. 83, p. 728, b 1–2. See p. 110 below.

2. See p. 55 above.

7. Be Yourself!

1. This question (which implies "What is your understanding of Zen?") is a standard expression used between Zen masters and their students.

2. *Nihon Shisō Taikei, No. 12: Dōgen* (The Works of Major Japanese Thinkers, No. 12: Dōgen), annotated by T. Terada and Y. Mizuno (Tokyo: Iwanami shoten, 1970), p. 469.

3. T. vol. 83, p. 728, b 19. Cf. Appendix 2.

4. A creative principle held by Bergson to be immanent in all organisms and responsible for evolution.

8. Reminiscences

1. See p. 2 above.

2. See p. 2 above.

3. Haya Akegarasu, *Shishiku* (Lion's Roar), ed. by Shūichi Maida (Nagano, Japan: Kaiun-dō, 1952).

4. See p. 101 below.

9. The Day Japan Lost the War

1. Shōtoku Taishi, *Nihon Shisō Taikei, No. 2: Shōtoku Taishi* (The Works of Major Japanese Thinkers, No. 2: Prince Shōtoku) (Tokyo: Iwanami shoten, 1975), pp. 11–23.

10. August 27

1. After the death of Akegarasu, the *Great Assembly*, his personal journal, was discontinued and a new journal by the name of *Kōsō* (Orchid) was started by his students.

2. Here Maida does not cite the one word that Akegarasu mentioned. Maida's following words might give us a clue for understanding the one word:

> Flaubert [1821–80, a French novelist] said, "There is only one word in the world that can accurately describe any one thing. The work of the novelist is to discover the word." Likewise, there is only one word in this world which can most adequately describe the "priceless jewel" at the heart of our being.
>
> My readers, please say the word. Please mention the word that everybody considers adequate here.
>
> I am delaying saying the word as much as possible and making my readers impatient. They may be thinking that I am enjoying tantalizing them.
>
> Now let me give my answer. Does it agree with your answer or not? I say it is "freedom."
>
> We are actually incredibly free. But the problem is that in spite of that, we convince ourselves that we are unfree. This is called upside-down-ness or deludedness. We can do whatever we want to do. We are inherently endowed with perfect freedom. Religion is recognizing the fact that we are free.

Even a person like Śākyamuni would not be able to think of any word that could better describe the "priceless jewel" than the word freedom.

> (Shūichi Maida, "A Priceless Jewel" in *Maida Shūichi Zenshū*, vol. 9, pp. 835–6)

11. Reflections on the Teacher-Student Relationship

1. T. vol. 82, p. 128, a 21–5.

2. Shōtoku Taishi, *Nihon Shisō Taikei, No. 2: Shōtoku Taishi*, p. 18.

3. T. vol. 82, pp. 239, c 28–240, a 1.

4. Cf. Shūichi Maida, *The Evil Person*, pp. 96–7.

5. See p. 110 below.

6. See p. 34 above.

7. See p. 97 below.

8. In the *Larger Sukhāvatīvyūha-sūtra* (T. vol. 12, pp. 266, c 23–267, a 13) fifty-three names of Buddhas are enumerated as the predecessors of the Buddha Lokeśvararāja, the teacher of the Bodhisattva Dharmākara.

12. Four Conditions for the Hundred-Eighty Degree Turn in Life

1. T. vol.83, p. 642, c 19–20.

2. *Shinjin datsuraku* (My body and mind have dropped off). Cf. Keiji Nishitani, *Religion and Nothingness*, pp. 184–93.

3. T. vol. 83, p. 733, a 25–6.

4. T. vol. 12, p. 267, b 24–5.

5. Matt. 7:7.

6. The passage Hōnen read was as follows: "Chant Amida's name single-mindedly and continuously, without paying any attention to the length of time whether you are walking, standing, sitting, or lying. This is called 'the action that will definitely lead you to liberation.'" T. vol. 37, p. 272, b 6–8.

7. Here Maida talks about an important experience he had in his early thirties, in which he, after searching a textual basis for his Buddhist ideas, finally identified it as the *Sutra of Impermanence* (T. 2, p. 2, a 2–11).

8. Cf. Daisetz Suzuki, *Myōkōnin* (Kyoto: Hōzōkan, 1976).

9. Shinran said, "The text that clearly shows the truth is the *Larger Sukhāvatīvyūha-sūtra.*" T. vol. 83, p. 589.

10. T. vol. 82, p. 1, a 11–2.

11. In the Pure Land tradition, the recitation of Amida's name or *Namu Amida Butsu* is called the Easy Practice, because it is believed to enable those of inferior potential (or the evil persons) to attain liberation immediately. It is contrasted with the Difficult Practices, religious practices such as the keeping of precepts, which those of superior potential undertake to attain Buddhahood. The doctrinal classification of the Easy Practice and the Difficult Practices was originally formulated by Nāgārjuna (ca. A.D. 150–250, a Mahāyāna thinker) in the "Chapter of the Easy Practice" in his *Daśabhūmi-vibhāsa-śāstra* (T. vol. 26, pp. 40–4). The Pure Land masters such as Hōnen and Shinran identified their tradition as the tradition of the Easy Practice.

12. *Byōjō-shin kore michi nari* (The flat-ordinary mind is the way). T. vol. 83, p. 642, c 19–20.

13. The Words of the Good Person

1. Cf. Appendix 2.

2. Kanzō Uchimura, *Uchimura Kanzō Shinkō Chosaku Zenshū* (The Complete Works of Kanzō Uchimura), vol. 16 (Tokyo: Kyōbunkan, 1964), pp. 130–2.

3. *Shin futaiten* (Genuine trust does not retrogress). According to Shinran, one who has attained genuine trust (*shinjin*) will certainly attain perfect nirvana immediately after his death; and his life in this world is characterized by non-retrogression, or continuous advance toward perfect nirvana.

14. "Even If I Were To Be Deceived"

1. T. vol., 82, p. 28, b 8. Besides "fallible" or "fallibility," *shaku* has other meanings such as "delusion," "illusion," "mistake," or "error."

2. *Shōbō-genzō Chūkai-zensho* (All Major Commentaries of the *Shōbō-genzō*), ed. by *Shōbō-genzō* Chūkai-zensho Kankōkai, vol. 1 (Tokyo: Nihon Bussho Kankōkai, 1956), p. 333.

3. T. vol. 83, p. 728, b 22–6. Cf. Appendix 2.

4. Ibid., p. 728, b 26–8. Cf. Appendix 2.

5. *Hirenzoku no renzoku* (a meeting of absolutely unique, separate entities), Dr. Kitarō Nishida's term. Cf. Kitarō Nishida, *Nishida Kitarō Zenshū*, vol. 8, pp. 7–71.

6. Shōtoku Taishi, *Hokke-gisho* (Commentary on the *Lotus Sutra*). T. vol. 56, p. 72, b 4–5. See p. 157 below.

7. Cf. Shūichi Maida, *The Evil Person*, p. 8.

15. "I, Shinran, Do Not Have Even a Single Disciple"

1. Cf. Shūichi Maida, *The Evil Person*, p. 21.

2. T. vol. 83, p. 609, c 11–3. Cf. Shūichi Maida, *The Evil Person*, p. 81.

16. The Negation of One's Teachership

1. T. vol. 83, p. 729, a 28–b 17.

2. Shōtoku Taishi, *Nihon Shisō Taikei, Vol. 2: Shōtoku Taishi*, p. 12.

3. T. vol. 83, p. 734, c 3–8.

4. Ibid., p. 734, c 21–22.

5. Ibid., p. 589, ab.

6. Ibid., p. 728, c 12–5. Cf. Appendix 2.

7. Zeami, *Kaden-sho* (Book for the Transmission of Flowers), (Tokyo: Iwanami shoten, 1927), p. 76.

17. Worship

1. Kitarō Nishida, *Nishida Kitarō Zenshū*, vol. 11, p. 289–468.

18. Self-Awakening

1. Kenji Miyazawa, "General Outline on the Art of Farmers" (*Nōmin geijutsu gairon*) in *Gendai Nihon Bungaku Zenshū*, vol. 24, (Tokyo: Chikuma shobō, 1954), p. 377.

2. See p. 34 above.

3. See Appendix 2 and pp. 106–9 above.

19. On History

1. See chap. 11, n. 2 (p. 90).

2. Kitarō Nishida, *Nishida Kitarō Zenshū*, vol. 9, p. 22.

3. Kenkō Yoshida, *Tsurezure-gusa* (Reflections in Hours of Idleness), (Tokyo: Iwanami shoten, 1928), p. 63.

20. Learn Freedom!

1. T. vol. 82, p. 1, a 15. Cf. Shūichi Maida, *The Evil Person*, p. 20.

2. Here Maida uses the term *jinen* (naturalness). Since *jinen* is synonymous with *Dharma* (the ultimate truth or reality), this translator uses "Dharma" as the translation of *jinen* from here to the end of this essay.

3. T. vol. 12, p. 267, b 29–c 2.

4. *Namu Fukashigi-Kō Nyorai* (I Bow to the Tathāgata of Inconceivable Light). This is called the nine-character Name or *nembutsu*. Cf. Shūichi Maida, *The Evil Person*, pp. 43–5.

21. Symphony of the Flame

1. Haya Akegarasu, *Akegarasu Haya Zenshū*, part two, vol. 2.

2. Ibid., p. 267. For the source of this statement, see Appendix 3.

3. T. vol. 83, p. 728, c 4–5. Cf. Appendix 2.

4. T. vol. 47, p. 452, b 17.

5. T. vol. 12, p. 267, a 24.

6. For the source of this statement, see Appendix 4. See also p. 55 above.

22. The Crucial Essence of Shinshū

1. The translator has abbreviated this title. The original title is *Senjaku Hongan Nembutsu-shū* (Passages Concerning the *Nembutsu*, Which Was

Chosen [by Amida] out of His Innermost Aspiration [To Liberate the Evil Person]). T. vol. 83, pp. 1–20.

2. T. vol. 83, p. 643, a 2–5.

3. See chap. 8, n. 3 (p. 69).

4. Cf. Appendix 4. For further discussion of this statement, see Shūichi Maida, *The Evil Person*, pp. 67–76.

5. Kitarō Nishida, *Nishida Kitarō Zenshū*, vol. 1, pp.1–200. Cf. Kitarō Nishida, *A Study of the Good*, trans. by V. H. Viglielmo (Tokyo: Print. Bureau, Japanese Government, 1960).

6. Ibid., vol. 2.

7. T. 56, p. 72, b 4–5.

8. *Nihon no Meicho, vol. 43: Kiyozawa Manshi, Suzuki Daisetsu* (Famous Books of Japan, vol. 43: Manshi Kiyozawa, Daisetz Suzuki), ed. by Mineo Hashimoto (Tokyo: Chūōkōron-sha, 1970), pp. 297–8.

9. T. vol. 84, p. 77, a 19–20.

10. T. vol. 83, p. 728, b 5. Cf. Shūichi Maida, *The Evil Person*, pp. 85–88.

11. Ibid., p. 728, b 5–7.

12. *Shinshū Seiten* (Kyoto: Higashi Honganji Shuppan-bu, 1970), p. 961.

13. Shōtoku Taishi, *Nihon no Meicho, vol. 2: Shōtoku Taishi* (Famous Books of Japan, vol. 2: Shōtoku Taishi), ed. by H. Nakamura, p. 424.

14. T. vol. 83, pp. 734, c 27–735, a 2.

15. For the meaning of the *nembutsu* (or *Namu-Amida-Butsu*), see p. 11 above. Cf. Shūichi Maida, *The Evil Person*, p. 8.

16. T. vol. 83, pp. 731, c 28–732, a 2. Cf. Shūichi Maida, *The Evil Person*, pp. 89–92.

17. *Yū* literally means "relaxed," "leisurely," or "calm." This term is not traditionally considered as a Buddhist or religious word. But Maida uses it as a synonym of nirvana, a term referring to perfect peace, which summarizes the essence of Buddhism. Cf. Shūichi Maida, "Religion of *Yū*" (*Yū no shūkyō*) in *Maida Shūichi Zenshū*, vol. 1, pp. 591–607.

18. *Poiesis*, a Greek word, meaning "activity of creating or making." Maida learned this concept from Dr. Kitarō Nishida. Cf. Kitarō Nishida, *Nishida Kitarō Zenshū*, vol. 10, pp. 124–76.

19. *Kanso* (simplicity) is generally not considered as a Buddhist or religious term. But Maida uses the term as a basic principle underlying the life-style of the true Buddhist. Maida wrote many articles on this concept. Cf. Shūichi Maida, *Kanso-ron* (On Simplicity) in *Maida Shūichi Zenshū*, vol. 2, pp. 169–263.

20. Cf. p. 115 above.

21. *Issoku ta, ta soku itsu* (The one is the many, the many are the one)—Dr. Kitarō Nishida's expression.

22. Cf. T. vol. 48, p. 294, c 12–5.

23. T. vol. 83, p. 730, a 5.

24. Ibid., p. 730, a 5–6.

Sources

1. "Meeting with Impermanence." In *Maida Shūichi Zenshū* (henceforth abbreviated as *MSZ*) [The Complete Works of Shūichi Maida], vol. 13, pp. 542–9. Nagano, Japan: Maida Shūichi Zenshū Kankōkai, 1969–71. The title of this essay is by this translator. It is part of Maida's transcribed talk entitled "Impermanence" [Mujō], which was given to the schoolteachers at Minami Minoa Grammar School in Kami Ina, Nagano, on February 8, 1966.

2. "The Most Important Thing in My Life." In *MSZ*, vol. 10, pp. 662–5. The title is by this translator. This essay is part of Maida's transcribed talk entitled "A Fresh Life" [Mizumizu-shiki inochi], which was given at the Myōtatsu-ji temple in Ishikawa Prefecture, on August 20, 1950.

3. "Standing-Death" [Tachi-ōjō]. In *MSZ*, vol. 11, pp. 469–72.

4. "Nothingness" [Mu]. In *MSZ*, vol. 7, pp. 361–2.

5. "Rev. Akegarasu and Rev. Kiyozawa" [Senshi to Kiyozawa-shi]. In *MSZ*, vol. 7, pp. 401–8.

6. "The December Fan Hall." In *MSZ*, vol. 7, p. 366. The title of this essay is by this translator. This untitled essay was written for the "Headland" [Misaki] section of the October 1956 issue of *Daisessen* (Mt. Himalaya), Maida's personal journal.

7. "Be Yourself!" The three short essays in this article were put together by this translator. (1) "The Teacher's Teaching" [Shikyō]. In *MSZ*, vol. 10, pp. 301–2. (2) "*Élan Vital*" [Eran vitāru]. In *MSZ*, vol. 7, pp. 377–8. (3) "Foreword of the First Issue of the Journal *Kōsō*" [Kantōgen]. In *MSZ*, vol. 11, p. 920.

8. "Reminiscences." All the titles in this article except "Flexible Mind" are by this translator. The first twelve fragments are excerpts from Maida's article "Rev. Akegarasu and Nagano" [Senshi to shinshū]. In *MSZ*, vol. 7, pp. 387–95. (13) "The Utmost Limit of Life" is a part of Maida's article "Midnight Summer Dream" [Manatsu no yo no yume]. In *MSZ*, vol. 7, pp. 383–6. (14) "Flexible Mind" [Jūnan-shin]. In *MSZ*, vol. 11, p. 590.

(15) "Speak Your Taste of It!" In *MSZ*, vol. 7, p. 380. This untitled essay was written for the "Smoke" [Kemuri] section of the October 1963 issue of *Daisessen*.

9. "The Day Japan Lost the War" [Haisen no hi]. In *MSZ*, vol. 11, pp. 114–5.

10. "August 27" [Hachigatsu nijū-shichi-nichi]. In *MSZ*, vol. 11, pp. 896–8.

11. "Reflections on the Teacher-Student Relationship." This article consists of excerpts from *MSZ*. These excerpts were made and titled by this translator. (1) "The Greatest Happiness." In *MSZ*, vol. 6, p. 509. (2) "Learn under a Teacher!" In *MSZ*, vol. 5, p. 572. (3) "The Dharma Flows between Persons." In *MSZ*, vol. 3, p. 648. (4) "Spiritual Communion." In *MSZ*, vol. 3, p. 754. (5) "Subjective Nothingness." In *MSZ*, vol. 2, pp. 165–6. (6) "Actual Experience." In *MSZ*, vol. 3, p. 729. (7) "Truth Negates." In *MSZ*, vol. 1, p. 594. (8) "Attaining Awakening Alone, without a Teacher." In *MSZ*, vol. 5, pp. 56–7.

12. "Four Conditions for the Hundred-Eighty Degree Turn in Life." In *MSZ*, vol. 9, pp. 876–80. The title and section numbers of this essay are by this translator. This essay is part of Maida's article "The Crucial Question in Life" [Jinsei no mondai]. In *MSZ*, vol. 9, pp. 865–80.

13. "The Words of the Good Person" [Yoki hito no ōse]. In *MSZ*, vol. 6, pp. 171–2.

14. "Even If I Were To Be Deceived" [Sukasare mairasete]. In *MSZ*, vol. 7, pp. 848–9.

15. "I, Shinran, Do Not Have Even a Single Disciple" [Deshi ichinin mo motazu]. In *MSZ*, vol. 9, pp. 724–5. This essay was published in the November 1952 issue of *Jippō* (Ten Directions), a Buddhist journal.

16. "The Negation of One's Teachership." In *MSZ*, vol. 6, pp. 135–40. The title of this essay is by this translator. This essay is chapter 6 in Maida's *A Study of the Tannishō* [Tannishō kenkyū]. In *MSZ*, vol. 6, pp. 87–162.

17. "Worship." In *MSZ*, vol. 9, p. 526. The title of this essay is by this translator. This untitled essay was written for the "Headland" section of the June 1957 issue of *Daisessen*.

18. "Self-Awakening" [Jikaku]. In *MSZ*, vol. 3, pp. 507–9. This essay is found in section 4 of Maida's "Commentary on the *Genjō-Kōan*." In *MSZ*, vol. 3, pp. 495–539.

19. "On History" [Rekishi ni tsuite]. In *MSZ*, vol. 8, pp. 741–2.

20. "Learn Freedom!" In *MSZ*, vol. 2, pp. 228–34. The title of this essay is by this translator. This essay is part of Maida's work *On Simplicity* [Kanso-ron]. In *MSZ*, vol. 2, pp. 171–263.

21. "Symphony of the Flame" [Kaen no uta]. In *MSZ*, vol. 7, pp. 349–58. This essay is a manuscript for a radio talk for Kanazawa Radio in Ishikawa Prefecture. This three-part talk was broadcasted on August 29, 30, and 31, 1959.

22. "The Crucial Essence of Shinshū" [Shinshū no kan'yo]. In *MSZ*, vol. 1, pp. 635–56. This article is chapter 3 of Maida's *Fundamental Dharma of the Buddha* [Shigen no buppō]. In *MSZ*, vol. 1, pp. 587–680.

Selected Bibliography

Works in Japanese

Akegarasu, Haya. *Akegarasu Haya Zenshū* [The Complete Works of Haya Akegarasu]. 24 vols. Ishikawa, Japan: Myōtatsu-ji, 1956–60.

Kiyozawa, Manshi. *Kiyozawa Manshi Zenshū* [The Complete Works of Manshi Kiyozawa]. 8 vols. Ed. by Haya Akegarasu and Kengyō Nishimura. Kyoto: Hōzōkan, 1953–57.

Maida, Shūichi. *Maida Shūichi Zenshū* [The Complete Works of Shūichi Maida]. 13 vols. Nagano, Japan: Maida Shūichi Zenshū Kankōkai, 1969–71.

Works in English

Akegarasu, Haya. *Shout of Buddha*. Trans. by Gyōkō Saitō and Joan Sweany. Chicago: Orchid Press, 1977.

Johnston, Gilbert. "Kiyozawa Manshi's Buddhist Faith and Its Relation to Modern Japanese Society." Unpublished Diss. Harvard University. Cambridge, Massachusetts: Harvard University, 1972.

Kiyozawa, Manshi. *December Fan: The Buddhist Essays of Manshi Kiyozawa*. Trans. by Nobuo Haneda. Kyoto: Higashi Honganji, 1984.

———. *Selected Essays of Manshi Kiyozawa*. Trans. by Kunji Tajima and Floyd Shacklock. Kyoto: The Bukkyō Bunka Society, 1936.

———. *The Skeleton of a Philosophy of Religion*. Tokyo: Sanseidō, 1893.

Maida, Shūichi. *The Evil Person: Essays on Shin Buddhism*. Trans. by Nobuo Haneda. Los Angeles: Higashi Honganji North American Translation Center, 1989.

Index